From Belfast to Peking, 1866–1869

From Belfast to Peking
1866–1869

A YOUNG IRISHMAN IN CHINA

Francis Knowles Porter

Edited, with an introduction by
J.L. MC CRACKEN

IRISH ACADEMIC PRESS

This book was typeset by
Woodcote Typesetters
in 11 on 13 pt Times for
IRISH ACADEMIC PRESS LTD
Kill Lane, Blackrock, Co. Dublin
and in North America by
IRISH ACADEMIC PRESS LTD
c/o International Specialized Book Services,
5804 NE Hassalo Street, Portland, OR 97213

ISBN 0–7165–2599–2

A catalogue record for this book is
available from the British Library.

Printed in Ireland by ßetaprint, Dublin

To Julie and Tricia

PREFACE

It is a hundred and seventeen years since Revd John Scott Porter transcribed into a leather-bound notebook the letters which his son Frank had written from China ten years before during his tragically short career as an official in the British legation at Peking. The collected letters were designed as a memorial to a much lamented son. Their publication perpetuates that memorial and at the same time provides a remarkably spontaneous and uninhibited commentary on a strange new world just opening up to Westerners. That publication has become possible after all these years is due to the generosity of Mr John Donnellan of Dublin who brought the document to the attention of the publisher and made it available for publication.

In recording my indebtedness to the people who have smoothed my path as editor I must first mention Dr Brian Trainor of the Ulster Historical Foundation who drew my attention to the existence of the letters and who has been supportive throughout. Sir John Horsbrugh Porter, Bart. and his son Alexander most generously saw to it that I was able to examine a collection of family photographs in the hope of finding one of Frank Porter. Unfortunately, as so often happens with family photographs, none was identified and such clues as there were to identification were inconclusive. Mrs Coleen Hardman of Harare, the Porter family historian, was a tower of strength in sorting out relationships and in other ways. To Andrew Wood of Durban who transformed my map I am indebted for an expertise which is beyond my ken. Mr Tom Moore of Belfast very kindly searched through the records of Revd John Scott Porter's church for information. My one-time student and all-time friend Anne Fay and my son Sean McCracken did sterling service in solving problems for me while I was out of Ireland. To staff in the following libraries, old friends and new acquaintances alike, I want to express my sincere thanks and great admiration for their patience, courtesy and diligent helpfulness: Belfast Central Library, Linenhall Library, Belfast, National Library of Ireland, Royal Irish Academy Library, Dublin and Irish Collection, Gilbert Library, Bray Public Library, Killie Campbell Africana Library, Durban, Don Africana Library, Durban, Durban Municipal

Reference Library. Finally, the lively interest which Mr Michael Adams of the Irish Academic Press has shown in the preparation of this book has added immeasurably to the pleasure of the task.

J.L. McCracken

CONTENTS

LIST OF ILLUSTRATIONS

INTRODUCTION

THE LETTER-WRITER AND HIS FAMILY

The author of these letters, Francis Knowles Porter, was a man in his early twenties, the son of Revd John Scott Porter, minister of First Presbyterian Church in Rosemary Street, Belfast, a non-subscribing presbyterian or unitarian congregation. His mother was the daughter of a Belfast doctor, Dr Andrew Marshall. Porter went to school at the Royal Belfast Academical Institution, across the road from his home in 16 College Square East, and then, at the beginning of the 1862 session, he embarked on an arts course in the Queen's College, Belfast. Three years later he graduated with a BA degree from the Queen's University in Ireland.

Like many other middle-class Irishmen of the day with ability and limited means he aspired to a post in a colonal administration. His first application, to the colonial office for leave to sit the examination for a writership in Ceylon, was unsuccessful, but when he applied to the foreign office he was selected as one of the eleven candidates chosen to compete for three places as a student interpreter attached to the British legation in Peking. Of the other two successful candidates one was a fellow student from Queen's College, Belfast. All three left for China on the same boat at the beginning of 1866.

In Peking the new student interpreters were housed in the complex of buildings rented by the British legation from a Chinese nobleman. They found four other students already there, two of them from Ireland. All were under the supervisions of Thomas Wade, Chinese secretary and chief secretary of the legation, who provided them with a series of exercises which he was preparing for publication. In addition, each student was assigned a Chinese teacher; Porter's teacher did not speak a word of English.

A year and a half after Porter's arrival in Peking an examination was held for three senior studentships. It was a three-day affair, conducted by John McLeavy Brown, assistant Chinese secretary, a Queen's College man, in the presence of Robert Hart, inspector-general of maritime customs in China, another Queen's graduate, a

Chinese scholar who had been Wade's teacher, and the ambassador, Sir Rutherford Alcock. Porter came first, a success which boosted his salary from £200 to £300 and earned him the privilege of staying longer in Peking, nearly another year, as it turned out. Then he was posted to the consulate at Ningpo.

The following Easter, at the beginning of April 1869, he and two friends went on an expedition up-river by boat. On the first evening Porter decided to have a bathe before going to bed; although his friends tried to dissuade him he dropped from the boat into the river. Presently a cry for help was heard but his companions were not able to rescue him.

For a better understanding of the letters it is necessary to know something about Frank Porter's family and background. When his father John Scott Porter was installed as minister of Rosemary Street congregation in 1832 the presbyterian church in Ireland had just experienced a schism. A long-standing controversy between the orthodox majority and an Arian or liberal group in the church came to a head in 1829 when the dissidents broke away to become non-subscribing presbyterians or unitarians. Porter's grandfather, Revd William Porter, minister of Limavady, was a leading protagonist on the unitarian side and became the first moderator of the new body. Like others of his kind his quarrel with the presbyterian establishment extended to politics; while they identified themselves with conservative politics he championed liberal causes, including catholic emancipation, the burning issue of his day.

All Revd William Porter's children adhered to his liberal principles though, like him, they did not participate actively in Irish politics. In addition to John Scott, two other sons became unitarian ministers, Classon at Larne and James Nixon at Carrickfergus and later at Warrington in England. Another son, William, as attorney general of the Cape Colony, distinguished himself as the initiator of a colour-blind franchise for the colony and the upholder of equality between the races in the eyes of the law; and a daughter married Francis Dalzell Finlay, founder of the *Northern Whig*, the Belfast newspaper which spoke for Ulster liberalism.

The politico-religious controversy did not end with the schism. The Academical Institution where Frank Porter went to school had a college department as well which the founders hoped would develop into a fully-fledged university. It was largely due to the campaign of the orthodox presbyterians against this institution that the Queen's College system was established instead in the 1840s. John Scott Porter, as a theology professor for non-subscribing presbyterians in the college and a friend of some of the doctrinally suspect professors was involved in the continuing controversy. He was also a prolific writer, preacher and debater on unitarian doctrine. He had other interests too: in literature and music, in the preservation of the Irish language, in promoting undenominational education, in charitable organisations, in the work of the Society for the Prevention of Cruelty to Animals. He was, in short, a well-known citizen in what was still, in spite of its industrial take-off, a relatively small town.[1] He was equally well known in English unitarian and liberal circles. His first ministry was to the Carter Lane congregation in the City of London, a heterodox and liberal congregation like his Belfast one. When in London he was also involved in running a school at Islington Green and amongst his pupils were men who subsequently became liberal MPs. The news of Frank's death reached John Scott Porter when he was staying in Birmingham with Joseph Chamberlain, a friend since his Carter Lane days, and the father of the famous Victorian-Edwardian statesman, Joseph Chamberlain.

Frank Porter was the fifth of a large family, all of whom figure in the letters. He was twenty-one years old in 1866. The eldest was Isabella (Bella), aged thirty-four, who was married to Andrew O'Driscoll Taylor (Sandy), a linen and yarn merchant. They lived at 6 Murray's Terrace which was intended to be part of College Square South but that side of the square was never completed. Sometimes Porter calls the Taylors the Terraceans. They had young children: he mentions Theodora, Amy, Fanny, Billy and Sandy. Next came Andrew, aged twenty-nine, who was called to the Irish bar in 1860 and was to become eventually master of the rolls in Ireland. Two other brothers were older than Frank: Willie, aged twenty-five, and John, aged twenty-three. Willie was abroad, at the Cape, and was a source of worry; John had just got a job in London. Younger than Frank were James, aged nineteen, Margaret (Maggie), aged seventeen, and Drummond, aged fifteen. James worked in a bank for a time but left and was eventually found a job abroad. Maggie had just finished school and Drummond was about to get his first job with a merchant.

Porter asks about, or says he is writing to, other relatives outside the immediate family circle: Aunt Finlay, his father's sister, her daughter Polly and her daughter-in-law Janet, his grandfather Dr Marshall

---

1 The population was about 121,000 in the early 1860s; thirty years before it had been only 53,000. Professional and business families like the Porters still lived in the heart of the town.

and his aunt Eliza, his mother's sister, and his second cousin Victoria (Tony), daughter of Revd John Porter of Belfast, and Mrs Nixon Porter, wife of Revd Nixon Porter of Warrington.

THE LETTERS

This is a collection of fifty-eight letters written by Frank Porter to his family between 7 January 1866 and 27 March 1869. Most by far are to his mother; the rest, with the exception of one each to his brothers Andrew, John and James, are to his father. Eleven letters were written during the seventy-day journey from Southampton to Peking, the remainder from places in China, mainly Peking.

The letters are at once a revealing insight into an individual personality and an enlightening commentary on a political situation at a crucial moment and from an unusual standpoint.

Porter emerges as an exuberant young man, deeply attached to his brothers and sisters, to his father and especially to his mother. He had a well-developed sense of humour, a friendly disposition and an inquiring mind. He was intelligent and observant without being pedantic in his comments. Yet he was sufficiently at home with Latin to produce the appropriate tag, he assiduously applied himself to mastering Chinese and he proposed to brush up his Latin and Greek and take up Hebrew as a diversion from his Chinese studies. He showed regard for scholarship and achievement but he could be amusingly disrespectful when writing of his elders and superiors. Attorney General William Porter and his friend Hugh Lynar are 'the Kaffir chieftains', an ex-governor of Hong Kong 'a hoary old sinner', the missionaries 'devil-dodgers', the ambassador Sir Rutherford Alcock 'the old boy' and a clerical colleague of his father in Belfast 'that slimy hypocrite Jellie'. His flippant and often unflattering remarks about foreigners should not necessarily be taken at their face value, and he was ready to acknowledge their good qualities, like the politeness of the Chinese. For a man who according to himself had no special bent he was remarkably wide-ranging in his observations and had a keen eye for detail. It was not only the grand and the bizarre that impressed him; he noticed and recorded as well such things as the flowers and trees he saw, the bird life or lack of it, the dress of people he came across and their attitude to strangers. Though he was not, as he said, particularly interested in politics he was forthright when he did comment on public affairs, whether it was the activities of the Fenians in Belfast or the sacking of the Summer Palace in Peking. And perhaps most important in the present context, Porter had the ability to write intimate, chatty and informative letters with a fluency and grace which add immeasurably to their impact.

A special historical significance attaches to these letters for two reasons. One is that they were written in the very early days of Western intrusion into China. Although the first Opium War had forced China to cede Hong Kong to the British and open five treaty ports to Western trade in 1842 it was not until after a second war that a final settlement was worked out. Lord Elgin's entry into Peking in 1861 took place a mere five years before Porter arrived. The cadet system under which he came out had been devised by Sir John Bowring, plenipotentiary and superintendent of trade and subsequently governor of Hong Kong, whom Porter knew. The first cadets arrived in 1862, four years before him. He came by the overland route through Egypt, for the Suez Canal was not opened till the year of his death. He was in regular contact with men who had played and were playing a key role in shaping British policy in China; the head of legation, Sir Rutherford Alcock, Thomas Wade, chief secretary of the legation and subsequently minister in succession to Alcock and Robert Hart, inspector general of Chinese maritime customs and trusted adviser of the imperial Chinese government. Wade and Hart made proposals to the Chinese government in 1865–66 about internal reforms, the introduction of Western technology and the necessity for diplomatic representation abroad. Porter witnessed and commented on some of the events which had great significance for the future, like the action of Robert Hart who took with him when he went on leave in 1866 a sixty-year-old Manchu, Pin-ch'un, and a few other officials on a sort of unofficial mission. Porter was well aware, too, of Chinese curiosity about the foreigners who had lately come among them and of their hostility to them, as shown when the ambassador's step-daughter was pelted as her carriage was leaving the races. At a more personal level the letters are revealing about the daily life and social activities of this first generation of British ex-patriots in the newly opened up China.

The other claim to uniqueness that can be made for these letters is that they were written by a young man to his family. Travellers, missionaries, soldiers and statesmen had written about China, and were to write about China in the future, from their particular professional standpoint, sometimes with publication in mind. Porter had no such idea. Nor had he any special expertise, experience or motivation. He said in one of his letters to his mother, 'Your news was just exactly of the kind that most interests me, local events that occur in your own sphere'. He tried to reciprocate. And since, as he said, 'so little is known about China at home that almost anything is acceptable,' he wrote about what he did and saw. When his father in the last year of his life copied out the letters it was not with any thought of publishing them. 'They are copied in this collected form', John Scott Porter wrote, 'to prevent the risk of the loss of any portion of what must be a very precious relick of one so warmly loved, so deeply regretted.' The letters were very private documents; therein lies their worth.

THE PORTER MANUSCRIPT

Memorials of
Francis K. Porter, Esq., A.B.
late Interpreter to
Her Britannic Majesty's
Consulate at Ningpo

With Letters written on his Voyage to China,
and during his residence there
and an Appendix
relating to his untimely Decease

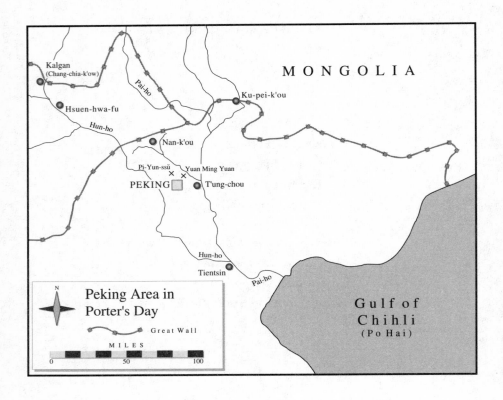

Kalgan
(Chang-chia-k'ow)

Pai-ho

MONGOLIA

Hsuen-hwa-fu

Ku-pei-k'ou

Hun-ho

Nan-k'ou

Pi-Yun-ssŭ   Yuan Ming Yuan
              ×   ×
PEKING □   T'ung-chou

Hun-ho

Tientsin

Pai-ho

Gulf of
Chihli
(Po Hai)

N

Peking Area in
Porter's Day

Great Wall

MILES

0   50   100

MEMORIALS

Francis Knowles Porter, the subject of the following Memoranda, fifth son of the Rev J. Scott Porter of Belfast, and his wife Margaret, daughter of Andrew Marshall MD, was born on the 8th of December 1845.

From an early age he showed marks of a lively, cheerful temperament combined with considerable ability, and a most affectionate disposition which greatly endeared him to his family and friends.

He secured his early education at home and in the Schools of the Royal Belfast Academical Institution; whence in the Autumn of 1862 he entered Queen's College, Belfast, as a Student in the Faculty of Arts.

There he pursued his studies during the regular undergraduate curriculum of three years; at the end of which he was admitted by the Senate of Queen's University in Ireland, to the degree of Bachelor of Arts, as appears by his Diploma dated the 11th of October 1865, and signed by the Right Honourable Mazière Brady, Lord Chancellor of Ireland and Vice-Chancellor of the University.

When he first entered College he had thoughts of studying with a view to the Ministry; but finding that the bent of his talent did not lie in that direction he soon devoted his mind in preparation for some secular employment, in which his attainments in language, literature and science might be available; and ultimately determined to procure, if possible, an appointment in the Civil Service. In this aim he was not at first successful. Having learned that there were a number of Writerships vacant in the Island of Ceylon which were to be filled by Competitive examination, he forwarded to Lord John Russell (afterwards Earl Russell), who was then Secretary of State for the Colonies, a letter with commendatory testimonials, requesting to be admitted to compete as one of the candidates; but received a reply stating that the number of candidates was limited, and had been filled up before his letter was sent in.

However, his Lordship added that a note had been made of his application, and that, along with others it would be considered as soon as any further vacancies occurred. No way disheartened by this disappointment, he soon afterwards forwarded a similar application to the Earl of Clarendon, Secretary of State for Foreign Affairs, in whose department it had been announced that there were vacancies for three young gentlemen, to be sent out to China as Student Interpreters; and who were to be employed, at first in connection with the British Legation in Peking; and afterwards wherever their services might be required. In this case he was more successful. He was selected by Lord Clarendon as one of eleven Candidates who were admitted to compete: and after a very minute and searching examination under the direction of the Civil Service Commissioners, he obtained the third place.

His Certificate of Competency from the Commissioners is dated on November 2nd 1865, and his warrant of appointment was forwarded by Lord Clarendon, with full instructions as to his further procedure, on the 14th of the same month.

Scarcely had he secured this prize when the chance of obtaining a still more valuable one presented itself. Agreeably to Lord John Russell's intimation a note of his former application to the Colonial Office had been made; and on the 21st of November a letter was received from Mr Cardwell, who had succeeded his Lordship as Secretary of State for the Colonies, stating that vacancies had occurred in the Civil Service in Ceylon; and that if he still desired to compete, he would be admitted to do so. On full consideration, however, Frank determined that it would be unwise to throw up an appointment already gained, after considerable effort, backed by the warm recommendation of persons of influence, in order to compete for another, which though more valuable in itself, he might not succeed in obtaining. Mr Cardwell's offer was therefore declined, with thanks.

As soon as it was known that he had been selected to fill a situation in the public service abroad, some of his friends who were members of the Masonic Institution suggested that it might be advantageous to him to be enrolled in that respectable body, members of which are to be found in every part of the world, whose advice and assistance might be of service upon occasion. He complied with the suggestion and was duly admitted a member of the craft, by the Ark Lodge No. X and was soon afterwards furnished by the Grand Masonic Lodge of Ireland, with a Certificate addressed to all the Right Worshipful Lodges and all Free Masons throughout the Universe requesting them to receive and recognize him as a brother. This Certificate he carefully preserved so long as he lived; but it does not appear from his correspondence that he ever had occasion to make use of it.

After some weeks spent in making the usual preparations for a distant voyage and a long absence from home, the bitter hour of departure at length arrived. It was impossible to avoid contemplating the possibility—alas, too fatally realized—that it might be a separation forever, in this life. In addition to other causes of depression, his eldest brother, Andrew, between whom and Frank there existed the fondest attachment had been for several weeks laid up in typhoid fever, from which his life was for some time thought to be in danger; and it was feared that parting from his beloved brother might prevent or retard his recovery. Happily that danger was averted; but still the hour was a sad and bitter one to all who loved him; most of all to the fond mother who loved him with more than an ordinary maternal love; but who, we trust has now rejoined him in a world where no partings can have place. He left home, laden with gifts and tokens of remembrance from kindred friends and comrades, and followed by earnest prayers for his health, happiness and welfare from all who knew him. His father accompanied him from Belfast to Southampton, the port of embarcation; and never has forgotten or can forget the sad pale look of farewell which was turned to him from the quarter-deck of the Peninsular and Oriental Company's steamship, the *Massilia*, as she steamed out of the harbour. She sailed on her voyage on the 4th of January, 1866. The other two gentlemen, who like himself had been successful in the competitive examination—Messrs Harvey and McKean (of whom the latter had been a fellow student with Frank in Queen's College, Belfast)—accompanied him in the same vessel, and occupied the same cabin on board the *Massilia*. Subsequent events will be best described in his own letters to his mother and other members of his family, by whom they have been carefully preserved. They are copied in this collected form, to prevent the risk of the loss of any portion of what must ever be a precious relick of one so warmly loved, so deeply regretted.

May 1879

J.S.P.

Since the foregoing pages were written, a brief notice of Frank's infancy and early boyhood, from the pen of his fond mother, has been found among her papers and is here subjoined as a sweet though mournful memory of her and him.

A MOTHER'S REMINISCENCES, 1869

December the 8th—What recollections rush upon my mind and seem to overwhelm me at the sight of that date! On the 8th of December 1845, my fifth son was born; my darling Franky. I see him as I saw him first;—a small bright healthy little fellow; contented and quiet; with every indication of enjoying that first of God's blessings, health. I had a nurse ready to come home to him; Mary-Anne McAulay—from the Glens of the County Antrim, beyond Glenarm: a fine specimen of an Irish nurse. She was extremely good-looking, with a fine complexion, fine dark eyes and hair and splendid teeth. She nursed him well, and he throve every hour after she came to him. She was no adept in singing; but finding that we wished her to sing to the child, and to make him lively and active, she used to lilt to him constantly old strains that she had learned in the Glens; often unmusical and out of tune; but always pleasing to her nurseling, who became extremely fond of her. He danced and pranced, and held out his little arms to her whenever she appeared or called to him. The same woman afterwards nursed two other children for us; but "Master Frank" was her darling. A proud woman she was of him. She used every morning to bring him down to the dining room after our breakfast just after he had been bathed and dressed: and what a proud mother I was to see his father take him and toss him up in the air, while the little creature screamed with laughter and delight! On more than one occasion the child looked so attractive that his father would say "I really *must* take him in to see Miss MacAdam"[1] (one of our nearest neighbours and a very dear friend) and away he would carry him, delighted to exhibit all his little tricks. At this time he had a bright rosy complexion (which never left him while alive); a small pouting mouth and coral lips; and when he smiled—which was almost constantly—his whole cheeks became dimpled. In fact his entire face smiled. His hair was of a golden hue, inclining to red; and in consequence of the way his fond nurse set it up on the top of his head, as well as of its beautiful hue and fine texture, he used to be called "the golden crested wren".

---

1 She lived at no. 18 with her brother James who owned the Soho factory in Townsend Street.

When he was only eight or nine months old, his father was once singing to him as he sat on his knee, an old ditty the burden of which was,

"Your silk and your satin, and calico cotton,"

(the child had got on a new calico frock) when, to our amazement, he instantly caught the sound, and repeated "*cottin*"! We fancied it was only an accidental imitation, and tried him over and over again; but always with the same result. In fact he took the greatest delight in repeating the word after us. From that time he was quite remarkable for his power of imitation. He walked at eleven months old; and was very active; always moving about; seldom crying, never fighting, never fretting.

When he was about sixteen months old he used to play a considerable part of every day in the room beside me; and his little tricks were delightful to witness. My dear father—who was very fond of the child and took great notice of him, used often to drive to our house in a gig. One day the little creature was sitting on a low window seat in the parlour of our house at Larne, whither we had gone for the summer; and I observed that he had got a bit of stick which he was using as a whip. Soon I heard his voice raised as if he was urging forward a horse, while he stamped with his feet, and lashed with the whip. "What are you doing, Franky?" I said. "Oh," he replied, "Pa-papa—gig!" (*Pa-papa* being the name given to his grandfather, and *Ma-mamma* to his grandmamma). On the same day he rolled off the window seat, and seemed to fall—but got up again and fell, rose once more, "What are you doing, dear?" I asked. "Dhrunk, dhrunk!" was the answer. After looking at the little fellow for a second or two I plainly perceived that he was giving a very good imitation of a drunk man. His nurse told me that he had seen a man in that condition, while she had him out for a walk on the previous day.

Even at that early age he was the favourite with his brothers. He was very independent in his ways, and would make himself happy under any circumstances. He was perfectly free from jealousy, and would part with or share anything he had.

When he was quite a small child, measles came into the house, and at that time there were a brother and a sister younger than he; they were all ill together, and some of them so severely that they had to be carried about the room in which they slept and up and down stairs almost constantly, and it was difficult to pacify the poor sick creatures, do what we might. Franky however kept perfectly calm and happy, and consequently his attendant left him pretty much to himself, being entirely engrossed with the rest. I observed that he was not in the room with the others, and I said "it is not fair to leave that poor darling quite alone;" so I went to the room in which he lay to see how he was getting on. The room was darkened, his eyes being very sore: but the little darling was lying in his cot, singing at the top of his voice! I never could forget it. It seemed to strike my conscience as such an unmerited return for the neglect with which he had been treated. "Darling child," I said to him, "how are you?" "Oh mama, quite well!" "Are you not very lonely?" "Oh no ma! I'm just singin!" "Do you want anything?" "Oh no ma, I do not." "Would you like anyone to come and sit with you?" "O ma, I would!" he replied with great eagerness. When I looked at him his eyes were closed and inflamed so that he could not open them; his skin was burning like a coal, and his pulse was flying.

The same cheerful uncomplaining spirit followed him in after years. The other boys would sometimes say to me in the morning, "Mama, I do not think Franky's well." Of course I examined him, and by dint of cross-questioning would find that he had a very sore throat, or some other ailment, which by most children of his age would have been made a great deal of. In general however he had fine health, and except in measles and whooping cough, I never had to nurse him through any serious illness.

When he was between four and five years of age, I commenced to teach him to read. He was a very apt scholar, always doing his best; and enjoyed learning, especially with his brothers. I often read stories to him and them, and a happy party we all were. I think I see their bright earnest faces turned eagerly on me, their happy mother! I taught them all to crochet and to sew a little; and long after they were mere children, they would have sat in the little parlour of our house at Larne, of a wet day, for hours, doing their little bits of work or trying to draw, while I read to them Sir Walter Scott's *Ivanhoe*, or some other of his delightful tales. I have now a small anti-macassar worked by Franky; one by John, and one by James. They are treasures, full of sweet memories to me!

When about six years of age, Franky began to take lessons regularly from his eldest sister, who taught him and James for about two years. His memory was remarkably good, and also his capacity for learning languages. His progress in French was astonishing, and his accent perfect; and this facility became greater every day. When he went to the Academical Institution, his French master said he pronounced like a native; and when he went out to China and had studied for a couple of years or so the language of that country (said to be the most difficult that is anywhere spoken), he was reckoned one of the very best speakers and writers of Chinese in connexion with the British Legation.

But I return to his power of memory. One day after dinner his sister said to him, "Now Franky, do you think you would venture to repeat your poetry to your papa, today?"—"Yes Bella; I think I can." So the book was brought (Macaulay's *Lays of Ancient Rome*): and that child—certainly not more than seven or eight years of age—repeated *with feeling*, and without being *once* prompted, the whole seventy long stanzas of the *Lay of Horatius*! He could not have been older than I have stated, for I perfectly recollect him standing before his proud father, in his chequered pinafore, with a frill round his neck, short white drawers, and chubby bare legs. His father gave him a shilling, and I believe that shilling afforded more real pleasure to both father and son than many hundreds of persons have felt at receiving thousands of pounds. He could at that time, repeat many more *Lays*: I recollect that of *Richard Coeur de Lion*. How he spent that shilling, I forget: but it certainly was not upon himself; for never did a boy spend less upon himself than he did. He never asked for money. When I offered a few pence, his reply often was, "Oh ma, I don't want it." Neither did he care for having money. Often I found his pocket full of school-tickets which he had earned by saying his lessons well, and for which he knew that his father would pay him in cash, if he had produced them at home. He liked to gain the tickets, but seldom asked for the price which was always given for a certain number of them. I often found dozens of these tickets in his drawer, which he had never exchanged for coin.

His eldest brother Andrew and he were devotedly fond of each other: Franky looking up to Andrew as to some superior being. He delighted in receiving messages for him, or doing any thing that kept him in his company. He used to follow him up to his room when he would be dressing to go to a party; and would be perfectly happy if allowed to remain in the room and attend upon him. In fact he said, "if Andrew would just allow him to be his little servant he would be contented and thankful." His delight was to carry his fishing-basket, or his rod, when he went to fish; or in fact to do anything, or run anywhere, for his beloved brother. Andrew could tell many little incidents that occurred about that time. His admiration was just as great for the brave, courageous generous and loving child as was the child's love and admiration for him.

It is lovely to recall these things. They are like sweet pictures whose beauty never fades. My boy is gone; but thank God I have those blessed memories of him still.

His school life was a happy one. He was a favourite with all his teachers and the delight of his school-fellows; many of whom entertained a strong and ardent affection for him while he lived, and sorrowed deeply for his loss. The Saturdays, when the boys got off from school at twelve o'clock, were always looked forward to with pleasure, and a party used to start off, for a game of cricket, or a long walk. He was generally with the walkers. They got their luncheon with them, and generally returned just in time for dinner after visiting Collin Glen, or the Cave Hill, or Divis Mountain or some other favourite resort. He had a particular relish for all natural objects, and a fine view of mountains or the seashore always gave him intense delight. His fondness for animals was remarkable: and he had the art of attaching them to himself, and of taming even wild birds with ease. On one occasion he set off from Larne with a young friend for a walk to Ballygally, which is a bold promontory overhanging the sea about three miles from home. His eye, always quick, perceived a hawk, flying in and out of a crevice in the face of the cliff. At the imminent risk of breaking his neck he climbed up a most dangerous way, and succeeded in bringing away two young hawks, covered with down. The mother bird flew past him, and past again, as if about to make a dart at his face; but nothing daunted, he descended from crag to crag, and brought his prize to his brothers in safety.

One of the birds he gave to his companion; the other he brought home and exhibited in triumph. That bird in a week would sit upon his finger and eat from his hand in the garden. When old enough to fly it would fly up and sit upon a tree; always coming to his finger again when he called "Veeliam's Pacha!" When the family returned to College Square the hawk once flew to the top of one of the adjoining houses, and we thought it was lost; but when he called it to him, holding up a bit of meat in his hand, it came . . .

[Left unfinished]

THE LETTERS OF FRANK PORTER

To his Mother

On board the *Massilia* at Sea—Monday January 7th 1866

My dear Mother,

I have not been able to do more in the way of keeping a Diary, than merely jotting down a line or two in my pocket book which I can enlarge at leisure; for the sea has been so rough and the ship so unsteady that writing has been almost impossible. I shall however tell you now how I have passed my time thus far, and in due time you shall have the journal written up.

On Thursday evening we got out into the channel, and fell in with very bad weather; "rain and much wind." I was therefore beastly sick, and ate nothing. However I got a little sleep that night and rose again on Friday; staid on deck all day, eating nothing and rolled up in my muffles. Towards evening I pulled up and took some tea and turned in to bed at 7 o'clock. On Saturday I awoke hungry and eat my breakfast and have since been quite well, and eating like a hippopotamus. The order of the day is as follows. At six o'clock in the morning the steward brings in to each person a cup of tea. At nine we breakfast. The band plays from ten till twelve, when we have lunch. At four dinner. At seven tea: and at nine grog. To the last meal, which is only a glass of "summut" and a biscuit I have not gone yet. I have been too sleepy and have turned in at eight.

The weather was fine on Friday, Saturday and Sunday and today it is lovely. We are now out of the Bay of Biscay, in which I was not sick—and on Wednesday evening we expect to be in Gibraltar, where I shall post this scrawl. The people on board have been all or nearly all ill; most of them worse than I was. Some have not yet left their berths. Captain Crawford is on board, and he and I fraternize a good deal. He is a very pleasant fellow, and it is a godsend to have someone to speak to. There are four or five newly married couples on board; but they are the most miserable looking wretches!—All of them seem to be permanently sick.

My novels are of great advantage even now: I do not know what I should do without them. So now you have an idea of how I pass my day. I feel very lonely sometimes, looking out upon the big sea, and not even a sail in sight! but that of course is to be expected, and the welcome sound of the trumpet calling to meals, generally dispels my gloom. I shall write from Malta an account of my visit to Gibraltar— and what I saw there; so good bye. Love to all at home.

Your ever loving Son,

Frank Porter

To his Mother

At Sea—January 9th 1866

My dear Mother

Since I wrote the above, we have come in sight of land; some part of Portugal between Lisbon and Cape St Vincent.

The weather continues beautiful and I feel already the change of temperature. The breeze today is directly with us—"Ventus a puppi" as we say in the Classics, and the sea is of the most delightful blue with large white breakers. Last night I stayed on deck till after eleven o'clock. The night was warm and balmy, and I could not go down to that close cabin, with three of the most inveterate snorers! The phosphorescence of the sea was the most brilliant thing you can imagine. The track of the ship was as it were delineated in fire!

We expect to be in Gibraltar at about seven o'clock tomorrow morning. We have been going today and yesterday at the rate of 11 knots an hour [*sic*]; before only 8 or 9. I feel very lonely sometimes; but that will wear off with time, and as I see more to occupy my mind. From Malta I shall write to Johnny; so you need not complain if there is no letter to you. The ladies on board are not nice: at least I do not think them so; but that may be because I have been all my life among those who are, and am consequently too particular! Please send one of my new photographs to Martha Taylor, whenever they come home—I promised her one. Give my love to all at home. Good bye.

Your loving son.

To his brother John

January 10th 1866

My last letter home was very hurried; my excuse was that I had nothing of interest sufficient to fill a letter; but today we have been into Gibraltar, and the account of it may be agreeable to you. We sighted land on Tuesday at about one o'clock; some part of Portugal off Cape St Vincent, and this morning at six o'clock we were going through the Strait of Gibraltar (nautically the *guts*). We were quite close to the coast of Africa at one time, and saw the mountains of Morocco. The whole view was the most splendid thing I ever saw. The morning was fine and the sky clear. (The mornings here are quite light now, at six o'clock.) We anchored in the harbour of Gibraltar, and went in to the town by boats. The distance is but half a mile, and we passed a great number of ships, lying there; among others HMS *Racoon* in which HRH Prince Alfred is. The noble prince came in a man-of-war's boat to our Steamer, and left some papers. I had a fine view of him. He is like the Prince of Wales, but more expression in his face; a fine broad shouldered chap, well bronzed by the sun. So much for him. On our arrival at the jetty we were besieged by guides, worse even than at the Causeway Hotel:[1] but I sent them to the right about shortly. The town is a good looking place, most beautifully situated; but the people are beastly. The men are short, yellow, sharp looking devils: and the women except for the colour of their eyes, are really very ugly. Not a tint of colour in their faces! They wear the mantilla with a high comb. Most of the people from their consistant intercourse with English people speak the language a little; but their own jargon is the most terrible thing to our ears, as their voices are high pitched and rough. I saw as much of the place as could well be done in three hours, for we were behind our time and could not stay any longer. The English troops are stationed in a large square in the centre of the town; and there are towers and look out-posts also full of them all round the rock. Fruit is very plentiful in the market. Pomegranates, grapes, apples and oranges were in profusion. I bought 50 splendid oranges for one shilling; and a basket to carry them cost 3d more. There are oranges on board; but when they can be had so cheap elsewhere, we would rather do that than keep running to ask every time we want one.

1 The guides at the Giant's Causeway in north Antrim were notorious for their persistence.

I send you a couple of photos. One is of Gibraltar; the view is from about the place where our ship lay at Anchor and is very good indeed. The other tells its own tale. Give it to James, he being fond of such spectacles.

The weather is most heavenly. Today was almost too warm, and the sky had not a cloud. the sea is as calm as a milk-pail. At night there is the most brilliant flashing phosphorescent light on the waves when they are broken by the paddle, like millions of floating stars.

We expect to arrive at Malta on Sunday morning, and from that I shall post this letter. I shall send from Alexandria an account of Malta and the doings there. Need I add that I am well and enjoying myself as well as I can in this confined area. They are getting up a danse tonight on deck, which has been well scrubbed, and canvas hung round the bulwarks to keep out the cool breeze. I suppose I must join the gay and festive throng, though I have no heart to do so. The ladies on board are not nice; and they are furthermore old; so I have no heart to foot it with any of them.

Tell my mother that this letter to you must be considered as to her also; for I cannot write two. You can tell her all that is in it. Short as it is, it would be even shorter, if the ship were not so steady. When she rocks there is no such thing as steady writing. Well I think I have told you all I can. In my next I shall have more incident to relate, probably; for we stop about nine hours at Malta, as we have to coal there. Give my love to my father and mother; to all the boys and to Maggie; also to Sandy and Bella; and with love to yourself, believe me, dear Johnny, Your loving brother,

P.S.—January 11th 1866. Since I wrote the above, I find that I have time to enlarge my account in many ways. I shall try to give you an idea of Gibraltar, which I find I have failed to convey in my former remarks. The town is built on the slope of the rock, and is very unlike any of our towns in architecture. The streets are narrow and the houses very high, with green outside shutters on all the windows—from many of which I saw slovenly looking dames smiling out—dirty faced, grinning yellow creatures they are. The shops though good are small and combine the sale of a multitude of different objects, like "the pigs, mousetraps and rabbits" of ancient Irish song. In many of the courts in front of private gardens there were orange trees laden with fruit in the open air. The fortifications extend all round the town, and to the very top of the rock and to the east of it. The cannon in the walls in front of which we were lying, are well placed to receive an enemy, and there are plenty of British troops here to work them. How pleasant it must be for the Spaniards to have their town in the possession of an enemy!

We sailed out of the harbour at noon, and were soon on our way to Malta. The wind this morning is in our favour, and the sails are all set. We are going now 11 knots an hour and expect to be in Malta on Sunday morning. The weather is delightful; and if it were not for the breeze today the sun would be too strong. I can fully understand the epithet blue applied to the Mediterranean. On a fine day it is the most intense blue I ever saw: and today the waves are white-capped as far as can be seen.

If you have any desire to know how we fare in the eating line, hear now. Breakfast is more like a dinner—fish, flesh and fowl in profusion, and curry and rice and all that sort of thing. Claret for breakfast (*drunk in tumblers*), for those who wish that beverage; and plain tea and coffee. Dinner is something gorgeous. Soup every day, and fish, wine good; but no *shampang*! I stick to the claret which is good, and not too heating in the warm days. With all this luxury there are certain discomforts attending sea life that are quite insurmountable. Four people in one small room not half the size of our little one at home, soon exhaust the air in it, and therein lies the chief draw-back. In the calm water, the port can be opened; but when the waves are at all high, or the wind on our side of the ship, the water comes in and wets the place. We have as fourth occupant of our cabin, a naval gentleman who is en route for Malta, to join the *Victoria* in the capacity of chief engineer. He is a vulgar dog of dirty habits; but withal, agreeable in his own way, and as we have him only for a few days more we can put up with him. Harvey is a decent enough sort of chap, who has seen a good deal of the world, and can make himself at home wherever he is. I shall not be sorry when landed safe at Shanghai for I am no man for the sea; and though at present I endure it I cannot say I enjoy it, except in this fine warm sunny weather. Love to all—

Your loving brother

2nd P.S.—I have nothing to add to my letter today (Saturday Jan 13) except that we have got into squally weather. Last night there was a terrific gale. The ship rocked backwards and forwards, and several of the passengers were sick who had quite recovered from the effects of the Channel and the Bay of Biscay. I am now quite accustomed to it and can eat my dinner unmoved even when the table is shaking like a swinging bridge. We expect to be in Malta early tomorrow morning and I shall in due time let you hear my first impressions about it. Today is beautifully fine, with the waves breaking against the boat; the wind from the west (which is in our favour) and all the sails are set. I really have nothing more to tell you; for the daily events of ship-life are very monotonous to me; and must be doubly uninteresting to one who only hears of them. Ever Yours

To his Mother
Wednesday, January 17th 1866

I hope that by this time you have got my letter from Gibraltar, and that Johnny has got the one I posted from Malta. We got into the latter place at 8 o'clock on Sunday morning: and as we had to coal the vessel lay in the harbour all day till Sunday evening. I went ashore of course, and went all over the place. Though it was Sunday the shops were all open and the people going about as if nothing like going to church ever entered their heads. I went in and saw the Church of St John which is a splendid building. Wherever gold and Mosaic work can be crammed on, they have it. There is a small organ more than 300 years old, which was brought from Rhodes. The ornamentation of the altar is in *lapis lazuli* as they told me. The natives of the place are ugly short black looking parties, who scorn the use of shoes (the lower classes I mean). The women wear a kind of black serge shawl over the head, which partially covers the face; they deserve thanks for the custom. You see I don't admire the distinguished foreigners I have seen. How will it be with the Pekinese? I forgot to tell you that the city is that of Valetta, on the north side of the island. I went up and saw the orange gardens belonging to the Government, who have them strictly watched by soldiers on guard. Oranges at Valetta are dear; 10d a dozen; so I bought no quantity. I could procure no photo views of any part of the island, or I should have sent you home one or two. I may get a view of Alexandria for you. The weather has been extremely rough since we left Malta. On Monday night we had a terrible gale. The waves poured over the deck fore and aft, and the noise was terrible. At dinner yesterday the smashing of crockery was ruinous. They have got wooden frames to strap to the tables on rough days, to keep the glasses and plates from rolling off; but even with these, half the things rolled into our laps. Numbers of passengers who had recovered are again in their beds. I can now laugh at the worst tossing of the boat, and McKean is also pretty well hardened to it; though on very rough day he does not venture down to dinner. We expect to be in Alexandria on Friday morning: for though we may arrive on Thursday night, it appears we cannot enter the harbour after 9 o'clock p.m. We are late: fourteen days voyage, instead of ten; but on Monday night we were only making two knots for the wind was right in our teeth. Today is fine but rough and I find it difficult to get even this short letter written, so great is the pitching of the vessel. I shall write you longer letters from Alexandria and Suez. You may perhaps wonder how my letters go to you. I post them on board the night before leaving any place: the bag is then made up and taken on shore to wait for the return steamer which brings it to Southampton. The postage that way is cheaper than sending them by land, though more tedious in arrival. You will be glad to know that I am perfectly well. Give my love to my father and the boys and Maggie, and believe me dear Mother, Your loving son.

P.S.—At Malta I got a bunch of the most lovely violets, which have scented my cabin ever since. I send you one or two lest my letter should "smell offensive in the eyes of your pure imagination".

To his Mother

Thursday, January 18th 1866

Today we are going on a great deal faster, and the wind has all gone down so that life is more enjoyable. At day-break the Steamer from Marseilles was descried about four miles behind us, and now she is ahead. If we had been in Egypt before her, we should have had to wait till she came but now both being together we shall just go slap through. (The *Simla* is the ship that takes us to Ceylon, and she will be quite ready for us at Suez.) We are to arrive at Alexandria tomorrow morning, and go over at once to Cairo: stop there for an hour, and then off to Suez and away the same night. At least so I am told. I shall write to you from the latter place, or from Aden. I am busy packing up my cabin articles today, and getting all my things together for my start. I send you a bill of fare which may interest you . I have no more to say except that I am your loving son

P.S.—I find that I took away, in the manner four of James' handkerchiefs. I fear there is no immediate prospect of his getting them back. Tell him that when "surrounded by oriental splendour" I shall send him costly shawls and scarfs of the most expensive silk—more I cannot.

To his Mother
Thursday evening, January 18th, 5 o'clock

Since I wrote the foregoing I have had the pleasure of seeing the lid knocked clean off my wooden box of books, and a dinge, not amounting exactly to a clean cut hole put in the side of the same! The luggage was being brought up on deck previous to being trans-shipped tomorrow, at Alexandria, and my trunk with others was handed up, with the lid only holding on by means of the wretched rope. One of the sailors put a stout rope round it and, round it again, which will hold it till I get on board the *Simla* when I may perhaps get a box at Cairo or Suez that will do to take things on. Several were absolutely thrown out on the deck. The sheepskin larger portmanteau is scuffed and bruised, but seems to hold well. Tell my father that if he ever sends another son by the same route he should give him trunks all leather.

Your loving son

To his Father
January 21st 1866

The last letter I wrote, brought me to within a day's sail to Alexandria: So now comes the history of my transit across Egypt. On Friday morning we got into the harbour of Alexandria, at about half-past seven. The town as seen from the sea presents nothing of interest and as we just rushed from the steam-tug which brought us ashore to the railway which was not 50 yards away we had no opportunity to see the sights of the place. At half past nine we left the station and were soon en route for Cairo. The appearance of the land from Alexandria to Cairo is like a cultivated model farm more than anything else. It is as flat as Flanders, is reported to be, and the inundation of the Nile seems to be very active in fertilizing the soil; for it has the appearance of being alluvial. We stopped for 20 minutes at some little town, about 60 miles from Alexandria, and lunched in the refreshment room. We got into Cairo at 4 p.m.: and as the hotels were all full (for the Pacha gave a fancy ball the other day, and the people from all parts of Egypt had crowded to it) we did not stay there at all, but went on to Suez. The desert begins just after leaving Cairo, and it fully deserves all the monstrous accounts given of it by travellers. For miles and miles one sees nothing but one smooth level map of brownish gritty sand with here and there at intervals of about a mile a thirsty looking plant. The rail-road is almost all downhill to Suez, but not withstanding the train only creeps along. We stopped again at a wretched little shanty in the middle of the desert to take *dinner*; which consisted of sea biscuit and blue mouldy Dutch cheese and the sourest and most bitter of beer. There was an alarm raised here that another train was coming up the line and though there is a telegraphic line the entire way, and a man at each of the stations to work it, some one had to be sent down on foot to see if the line was clear. This delay lasted for *five hours*! during which I am glad to say I slept comfortably. The sun during the day had been warm, but the night came on piercingly cold, and I was glad to wrap myself up in my great-coat and use half of McKean's rug for my knees. We got away at last, and arrived in Suez at 3 o'clock on Saturday morning at the quay, where we just walked on board a tug, and went to the *Simla* which was lying a mile and a half out in the bay. We got on board without any other adventure than a collision with a coal schooner, whose bowsprit and bows we tore away; whereupon ensued a tremendous scene of cursing and swearing in Arabic or Coptic or some such heathenish language, and a great deal of gesticulation from the commanders on both sides. At about 4 a.m. we were on board the *Simla*, where a hot supper was awaiting us: after which I turned into bed, where I lay till twelve o'clock. They would not have had us on board so soon but that the hotels at Suez are also fully occupied. So here is Sunday and we are still lying in the Gulf. The luggage is come on board today, and on opening my wooden box I find that three pairs of boots (new), have been stolen as well as three pairs of white ducks, and all my linen waistcoats except one. All the rest seem to be in the same condition as when packed. I opened the box in my cabin today in presence of McKean, and when I discovered the loss, I went at once to the purser of the ship, and brought him down. I shewed him the list of articles made out (fortunately) in my mother's hand-writing, and shewed him the box. He sent for the Conductor of luggage who is employed by the P. and O. Compy to watch passengers' luggage across Egypt, and the latter told me to apply for restoration to the first of the Com's Agents whom I may see at any of the ports I stop at. The boots are the greatest loss I could have had, for I have no way to replace them. They have only taken two pair; but of those they have taken one pair consisting of two right-foot boots of different pairs, one of them the extra-solid, the other the lighter; besides the pair of medium soled. So you might get McCollum to make me a right-foot solid boot and one right-foot, lightest sole, same as he made before, and they can come out first chance. If you would write to Mr Davidson, and tell him what I have lost, he might get the money refunded, or it might come out of the insurance. I am going to write to the first officer of the *Massilia* to enquire of the men who roped the box, if the articles were in it when they delivered it off the steamer. If I get a certificate from him to that effect, the Transit Co are the responsible parties. But let us have no more of this.

Monday, January 22nd—The *Simla* left Suez harbour yesterday at 2 o'clock and today we are fairly out of the Gulf of Suez and into the Red Sea. The weather is most heavenly and there is just enough of a breeze to render the strong heat endurable. We are going 11 knots and the steam is not yet up to its full pitch. Our crew is decidedly a mixed assembly; the greater number are Bengalees; there are also some Cingalese, and last, but not least six Chinese. The Chinese seem to be the ship's carpenters, for I see them going about with tools, hammering and cutting. They are extremely intelligent-looking fellows; all of them with dead black hair; and the pig-tails instead of being long, are plaited short at the back of the head. Their jargon is less offensive to the ear than the printed specimens of it are to the eye. They cannot speak a word of English. The Marseilles boat brought a great increase to the number of passengers. We are now about 200. Some of them are very nice people. At Gibraltar we took in three Spaniards of the Spanish navy. One of them—a fine old fellow—is an Admiral; the other two are a Captain and a Lieutenant. The Lieutenant speaks French, and by this means I have been of some use to them in getting them what they wanted at meals; for not one of them can speak a syllable of English. I speak French with the young fellow very often; and there is sometimes a hearty laugh from both of us when one is stuck for want of a word and the other cannot help him. There is on board a Mr. Gabbin, a man of about fifty with a very pretty young wife and a niece who is a widow. He found out from me by accident that I was a relative of the

Attorney General at the Cape, whom he knows. He saw his likeness in my album and recognized him at once. I was introduced to the two young females, and have been presented with likenesses of them all. His first wife, he tells me, was a Miss Battersby, whose family from the north of Ireland he says my uncle knows very well. You may perhaps have heard of them. I am very comfortable on board. We are all three in the same cabin again: and we have for fourth tenant, a navy surgeon, Dr. Roche, a Dublin man who is quite friendly, and inclined to accommodate in every way he can. I need not say that "I reciprocate the sentiment." My cabin is not far off the baths, and I have a salt-water sponge bath every morning. McKean bought a splendid sponge, larger than his own head, at Malta; and as he does not bathe he has placed the use of it at my disposal. There is some talk of private theatricals (or rather public), on board; but I do not join in any of those innocent amusements except as a spectator. They say that the *Simla* is famous for its theatricals.

And now I have to record with pain the loss of an article of as great necessity as the boots, and certainly one more valuable; namely the entire parcel of silver spoons and forks! They may have been put in the large leather portmanteau; if so, they are safe—but I have not yet had a chance of looking into it. On next baggage day I shall have it up from the hold, and examine the contents. I am however nearly quite certain they were put into the trunk. I have taken every book out of the latter, and they are not there. The knives and carvers and all my books and pistols in the trunk are quite safe, and I have it in my cabin so that nothing more can be stolen, till we get to Galle. In the meantime, I shall have it more securely lashed, and the lock nailed down. Does my mother recollect whether the spoons etc were in the portmanteau, or in the box? Fortunately as my money has scarcely been touched yet, I can buy in China a spoon and fork which will keep me going till I can have the means of buying more. My journey across Egypt you know cost me nothing except a trifle for lunch. Even with the loss of my precious boots and spoons, I am not cast down. The fine weather has an exhilarating effect that dispels gloom. I know at least that they were lost through no fault of mine, for I could not keep that heavy box under my eye all the time; so you may consider what is best to be done, and let me know. In the mean time, I shall take the advice of the luggage conductor, and claim from the first P and O Agent that I meet, the full amount of my loss: say £10 counting the smashed box at £3. The thing to be looked at is not the actual cost of the articles but how much it will take to replace them, even if it be possible to replace them at all.

Wednesday, January 24th—Today we are going along famously, for
the steam is now well up, and the sea is as smooth as oil. The heat is
oppressive, and the continual white glare from the sea and land is very
distressing. Tell my dear mother that I have mounted the blue veil,
which is a great comfort indeed; as good as a pair of blue spectacles
which are highly recommended for travellers, by the Red Sea. We are
to reach Aden tomorrow; and as the ship coals there, we shall have
time for a ride on a dromedary, which I understand is the correct thing
for English tourists. My letter will be posted at Aden; so I cannot now
give you any account of that place. In my letter from Galle I shall tell
you all about it.

So now with profuse apologies for the length of this epistle, and
for the irregular way in which the pages are arranged, (the result of an
accident) I find that I had better close the envelope. Give my best love
to my dearest mother, and to all the boys, and to Maggie, who I suppose
is back at Hampstead. I should have written to Andrew but my news
would have been exactly the same as what you have here, and the one
letter can serve for both. So now, dear Father, good bye. Remember
me to all the kind friends at Green Island;[1] and believe me ever your
loving son,

Friday, January 26th—We are a day later in arriving at Aden than was
expected, and I may as well tell you, that we are just now (11 o'clock
a.m.) about to enter the harbour. We are out of the Red Sea, and the
sun is still as warm as it was, though there is a strong breeze. The sea
too instead of being very calm is now running very high and the ship
has begun to roll a good deal. I hope that you have got all my previous
letters which were posted at Gibralta, Malta and Alexandria. The
shaking of the ship is so bad that I can scarcely hold my pen, as you
will perceive by the handwriting. I have nothing more to add but that
I am in excellent health and wish heartily that I was at Peking. Sea life
is not the sort of thing that I like. In eight days after leaving Aden, we
arrive at Galle—where we are likely to remain at least a night before
leaving in the steamer for China. I can therefore in my next letter tell
both of my voyage to, and arrival at that place; which I have not yet
been able to do. I shall there make the application to the P and O Agent
about the lost articles and try what can be done. Love again to all at
home from your loving son

1 Both his grandfather and his parents' friends the Allens lived at Greenisland on the
  north shore of Belfast Lough. William John Campbell Allen, 1810–84, called to
  Irish bar 1835, honorary secretary Royal Belfast Academical Institution, registrar
  of Queen's College for two years, was one of the most eminent men in Belfast.

To his brother Andrew
Saturday, February 3rd 1866

I was my intention to have written to you from Alexandria, and my mother has told you the reason I suppose, why I did not. My last letter brought me up to within half an hour of landing at Aden; and now to resume the narrative.

We all went ashore at Aden, and as the vessel had to take in coals, we stayed there a long time. But there was nothing to be seen. It is the most wretched place that can be. The station where the ships anchor is about three miles from the town. I took a horse (though it was in Arabia, I doubt much if it was "an Arab steed") and rode over to the place: but it was just as bad.

There is a regiment stationed there and so there was someone to talk to, for the officers are glad enough to see a new face. The natives there were not pure Arabs. They are more like the dirty Egyptians of Suez. I saw some Arabs however: fine looking tall, handsome men, with black moustache and beard, and very picturesque dress; white turbans, red tunic, red scarf, and long white mantle. After seeing all that could be seen, we steamed away at 9 p.m. I was going to bathe in the harbour of Aden, but on hearing that it swarmed with enormous sharks, I thought I could serve my country and my own interests better by living for a few years more. Since we left the latter place we have seen no land up till the present time. The heat has been very great, and the water as calm as glass. We see flying fish by the thousand—*literally*—they spring up from the ship's side, and skim along the sea, like swallows for about 100 yards when they drop in with a splash. There have also been porpoises playing about the bows of the ship. We have had much more gaiety on board this ship than in the *Massilia*. Dancing goes on nearly every night. Some of the passengers, assisted by the officers got up a theatrical performance the other evening, and played a couple of farces very well.

We have had real tropical weather since we left Suez, and brilliant moonlight every night. You have no idea of the beauty of the nights here. We can absolutely *read* by moonlight and generally take a nap in the middle of the day, when the sun is so powerful that you cannot play on deck (though they have up an awning) and stay on deck till twelve or one o'clock in the evening. The fore-castle is the coolest place in the ship: and thither I repair. The sailors sing and play (concertina, bones, and fiddles) every night; and some of them are very good musicians.

Sunday February 4th—We have this morning got into Galle harbour, I have not yet gone on shore; but as soon as I can finish this I am off. The town of Galle is very lovely, as I see if from the steamer. The cocoa trees grow down to the very water's edge. The water looks so cool and clear that I am almost tempted to risk my life for a bath; but that does not pay here, where there are sharks at every square yard.

3 p.m.—I have been over to the China Steamer, the *Baroda*, which takes us to Hong Kong, and have seen my luggage snugly put on board. She is a very fine boat, nearly as large as the *Simla*, and quite as well fitted up. She came from Bombay to Galle, where she takes the overland passengers, and starts tomorrow at ten a.m. I shall sleep on board tonight and be ready to go away at any hour in the morning, though most of the men on board prefer to pay for hotel accommodation. I have been all round the place, and find that it looks much better at a distance. The natives are hideous creatures. They are of a sort of bronze colour, and as they wear only one garment and that of no great dimensions, their skin can be seen to great advantage. They are little, ugly squat fellows: but strongly enough made. There are very few passengers going on to Hong Kong; but I understand we shall take up a lot more at Penang and Sincapore. My cabin has not yet been allotted to me, so I don't know what company I shall have. Tell my mother that I got from one of the stewards a brandy case, a strong box hooped with iron, to which I transferred my books from the lame trunk and left him the latter to make what use he can of: so I expect no more accidents to luggage till I arrive at Peking. The weather is delightful; if anything too warm. There has not fallen a drop of rain since we left Suez. I myself am quite well and in excellent spirits. I enjoy the novelty of the different sights, and I manage to get on as well as most of the people I see. Your books have been a perfect boon to me on the voyage. I really do not know how I should have got on without them. Give my love to my mother and father (and shew them this letter): and to the boys and Bella, and Sandy and believe me,

Your loving brother

To his Mother
Friday February 9th 1866

Faithful to my promise, I have up till this time posted a letter home at every place we stopped: and I shall continue to do so till arriving at Peking. I say this in case any of them should go astray. If you [saw] the interior of some of the post offices at those places, you would not be at all surprised at such an apprehension. The post office and the chief hotel seem to be the resorts of all the idlers and newsmongers. Any one can stroll in behind the counter of the former and stay there, chatting to the officials (who are natives), and smoking a quiet cigar, handling the letters the while. In spite of this however, my letters are not likely to go astray, as they don't contain money. I have only written one letter home from each place, for I really cannot find original matter for more, and I know that my letters are the baldest most miserable things that ever went by the name; but unless I told you the humdrum routine of every day (and all days here are alike) I could not make a letter of any decent length, to say nothing [to] interest you.

We stayed at Galle over Sunday night, which was unexpected; and steamed out of the harbour at 10 o'clock. The *Simla* started at the same minute for Madras: so we went out together. It was rather a nice sight, to see two big steamers going off with not more than 200 yards between them, but the *Simla*, though the oldest ship in the P & O Comp's fleet, is the fastest, and soon left us behind. The steamers instead of going up to Madras by the west coast of the island, go always by the east, to avoid some reefs, or something on the coast of Malabar, so we went in the same track for about 50 miles. The *Baroda* is superior in accommodation to anything I have yet seen. The fittings all over the ship are the best and most expensive of their kind. The wash-hand basins and bath are of marble; and the same elegance pervades every part of the vessel. Add to this, that the cookery is superior to that of either of the other two steamers and that I have a whole cabin to myself, and you may form a distant idea of my comfort. There are only 35 passengers on board as yet, but we may take in some Malays or other *nice* people at Penang or Sincapore.

Before going farther, a word or two about Ceylon. The first thing that strikes one is the profusion of vegetation. The trees are absolutely growing into the sea. I never saw anything like it and the farther you go inland, it only increases. The cocoa nut tree is the chief one in this part of the islands, there were also nutmeg and cinnamon trees. We got pine-apples, bananas and a fruit called *pomĕlos* (so pronounced), like an orange but about the size of my head, and with red flesh, and a green rind: also green oranges; and I saw some *yams* for sale. The people were like the usual run of beastly Easterns. I was sorry to leave such a beautiful place for I had not had my foot on anything like fresh grass for a long time. We ran races, and jumped to an alarming extent (in the cool of the evening of course)—and made ourselves so stiff that I for one have had no desire for active exercise since. Since we left Suez we have not had a drop of rain. It is the most delightful weather imaginable. On land it would be too warm: but we have a breeze here and cool air at all hours of the day and night; and as the sea is quite calm, the windows in the cabins are open all night. I call them windows: for the ships on this side have windows, two feet square: not the wretched little ports that we had in the *Massilia*. The officers in this ship are more accessible than the former ones. They join more with us passengers; perhaps because there are fewer of the latter. There is only one lady on board—fortunately for her she is married, and so does not give any annoyances. The unmarried ladies on board ship receive so much attention from the officers and passengers, that in about a week they become intolerable. I was watching with interest the progress of a flirtation on board the *Simla*, between a gallant major in the army and a widow with two encumbrances, both going to Calcutta. It must either be corrected by matrimony or an action for breach of promise: probably the latter. The crew of this vessel are altogether barbarian, except two quartermasters and the stewards (if they are part of the crew). The Hindoos awake me nearly every morning, by chanting oriental dirges on the decks, just overhead in loud harsh voices. I suppose they intend it for music; perhaps a morning hymn. But the mornings are so fine that I forgive them their wicked intentions. I take a bath at six in the morning and then walk on deck in my dressing gown and bare feet, till the first trump sounds for warning to breakfast. In the hurry and confusion of changing steamers at Galle, I got no washing done: but at Sincapore where we are sure to stay eight hours I shall direct my steward to give out some things. I saw the style of washing at Ceylon. All along the river's edge (there is a small river there) there are larger flat stones like pedestals for statue, firmly fixed half in and half out of the water. The natives then go to the stream and soap both the surface of the stone and the article to be washed. The next move is to seize the latter by both hands and smack it down upon the block, about fifty times as hard as they can, the article is then washed. The buttons must be either smashed or torn forcibly out. I already tremble for my shirts!

If I saw John Chinaman using my clothes in such a manner, I think I should shoot him at once!

I have been looking out for a shark ever since we came into the Indian Ocean, but hitherto without success. The officers tell me that they have been known to follow a vessel from harbour and keep in her wake for a fortnight. In such a case it is dangerous to fall overboard. The flying fish are still seen in numbers every day: they are larger here than any I have yet seen, and more numerous. We spring a covey of them about every half hour. I have seen a hundred or more all rise together. They have them dried on board and they are eaten like sprats at home. In this state they go by the name of *Bombay ducks*. They are like salt cow-hide, if you can imagine that. Some of the men relish them: I can't eat them. We have on board two cows, a lot of sheep and lambs; pigs, cocks and hens; geese, turkeys, ducks and pigeons; so we are well off for animal food. My principal drink on board is iced water, which I take at breakfast, lunch and tea. When the beer has been put on ice, I take it for dinner, and claret and water at supper. The beer I regret to say, is as often at blood heat as at any other temperature; and even when iced, if not drunk in five minutes after being opened, it grows quite warm: so you see that while you are putting your beer and porter inside the fender to take off the chill, I am crying out that I cannot get it cold enough. And yet with all this novelty and sight-seeing I am heartily tired of the voyage and wish I was safe at Peking. We are to get in Penang on Sunday morning, and Sincapore some day next week but we shall not be in Hong Kong till past the middle of the month. We are to be understood as having made a good passage to Shanghai if we arrive there some time in the first week of March. How long we stay there I don't know but we may count ourselves well off if we are at Peking by the first of April. Of the latter place the accounts that I have lately heard vary very much. One man says it is a jolly place, lots of sport, fine fun, good scenery, pleasant country and very cheap. The next fellow says it is a dull, dirty, miserable hole; no fun, dirty people as dear as death and all that sort of thing. I am inclined to take the former view of it. Where are respectable English people, one can never be destitute of enjoyment except under very peculiar circumstances. This however all remains to be seen. In the meantime I am prepared to put up with any minor inconveniences that must arise to a person going for the first time into a strange country; and that's the best sort of way to go to it after all.

By way of drawing to a close this epistle, I shall tell you that I am in perfect health and strength. The hot sun out here has played the mischief with me though: I am already burned worse than I ever was at the end of summer. When I wear my ring (*your* ring) on my little finger there is the mark of it in white, just as Maggie's cheeks with the strings of her hat at home. Still it is a healthy colour and that's my consolation. It is better than some of the colours that the men burn here sometimes. I have seen them as red as lobsters and the skin coming off their face!

The ship is infested with cockroaches and rats. I never knew what perfection cock-roaches could attain (physically) till I saw those monsters. I have killed some specimens at least three inches long! Fortunately we [are] free from annoyances of a worse kind. The rats run rampant through the ship; and as far as I can see, no means are taken to put them down. The ship possesses neither dog nor cat. Oh, for Charley, Jack, Tommy, Toby, Fly or any of the race of terriers that I have been accustomed to look up to with pride and veneration for the last five years! One short hour of any of those worthies, and the rats would fly the ship (such as survived) at the nearest port. By the way, talking of dogs ask James to go to Jack Pemberthy, and ask him for a likeness of "ee Dzack" as Fanny used to call him, and send it out to me as soon as he can. I shall write to James whenever I have time, and material to compose a letter of tolerable length, probably from Hong Kong, if not sooner.

The Spaniards continue to be very friendly with me by reason of my little assistance to them at first. They are all quite interested in teaching me Spanish. One of them has given me a little book of Spanish domestic phrases and their English equivalents which serves as a guide to students of either language. I can understand the ordinary phrases of salutation and such like, and the names of principal articles of food. They are going from Hong Kong to Manilla and I should not wonder if it be with some intention of going to Chili, or to be ready when called on to go. I shall be sorry to part with them for they have been as kind as people can be.

And now dear Mother, this letter must come to an end. I shall post it at Penang and another at Sincapore. My best love to my father, Andrew, the boys, Bella and Sandy and Maggie. When I get settled at the big city, I shall write to them all. Don't forget to remember me to Mary and Jane.[1] You might do this also as a favour if I inadvertently forget to mention them in any future letter to you: and if your conscience will allow you. So now goodbye. Believe me,

Ever your loving son

1 Most probably the family maids.

To his Mother

February 11th 1866

I have been told that my letter posted yesterday at Penang and this which I shall post at Sincapore will both reach you at the same time, because the homeward Mail had left Penang before we got in: but as this one is a couple of days' news in advance you won't object to have them both.

We got into Penang yesterday at seven in the morning. I swallowed my breakfast and went ashore with three other fellows. We were advised by the officers on board, after seeing the town to go to the waterfall in the neighbourhood, which we accordingly did. As the Captain only gave us till half past one on shore, were obliged to drive to the place. The drive was most delightful. The day was fine but not too warm; and the windows of the fly were all open. The scenery is every where beautiful. Just behind the town the island rises up very high and the hills are covered with trees, thick to the very top. The waterfall is about 120 feet high and it must be a grand sight in the rainy season. Yesterday there was not very much water. I send you a photograph of it, but it will give you a very poor idea of the beauty of the place. I tried to get cartes of the town and harbour, but could not. The variety of trees and plants was something astonishing to my weak nerves. Cocoas, nutmeg, cinnamon, plantain and coffee trees we saw all growing in a space of 50 yards square. The hedges are full of the most lovely flowers. There was a wild convolvulus (evidently a rank weed here), the flower of which was as large as a breakfast saucer.

I trampled on a plant which I saw growing all about here, and discovered the sensitive plant! no hot-house required for it here. What struck me most of all was the absence of birds. Except a kind of kite, with a white head and neck,[1] and the domestic sparrow I saw not a single bird. But the insects were most gorgeous. Butterflies as large as swallows: that is to say their wings when spread out extend as far. Without going on any more about its individual beauties, it is altogether the most lovely place I ever saw. I thought Galle was good, but it is not a patch upon Penang. It was just my idea of a tropical island. And yet it seems to be doomed that those lovely places should be inhabited by the most filthy people. Half of the inhabitants were Chinese, and the rest were—I don't know what—something very bad. We took four or five more passengers on board here; but none of them has been billeted

1 Brahming kite.

upon me; so I still have my cabin to myself. I really have no more news to give you, I think. We get into Sincapore tomorrow; and if we stay there any time I can tell you in this letter of my arrival there: so with that in view I shall keep my letter open.

Thursday, February 14th—We got into Sincapore harbour yesterday and were on shore at 11 a.m. The P and O Co's landing and coaling wharfs are four miles away from the town, so we drove in. Sincapore is not nearly as nice or as interesting as Galle or Penang. I was not much pleased with anything I saw, and that seems to be the general verdict against the place. The Malays are the natives: but for one of them you see 20 Chinese; the latter have completely established themselves here, and I should say, so much the better for Sincapore, for one of them can work down ten Malays. We walked out of the town, to see the residence of the Russian Consul. I was with Mr Baker who is in the Chinese Custom house at Tientsin, and he knew Wampoo the Consul, so got permission to see his grounds. They are tastefully laid out and the flowers and plants are quite new to me. It was a good way of passing a couple of hours. The steamer stays 24 hours here, starting at noon today and we make Hong Kong in eight days. Today is Valentine's day at home, and the Chinese New Year's day here. The Chinese were in an awful state last night, firing rusty blunderbusses, beating cymbals and tom-toms, shouting and sending up sky rockets to usher in the day with proper respect. I got you a photograph of the place. We are at present lying away to the left of the picture. I send you home these pictures, not that they can by any means interest you, but as something to show that I have been there. We took several passengers on board at Penang, and some are also coming today. The scenery going down the straits was very beautiful. We had land in sight, always on one, sometimes on both sides. There are little green islands about here, with trees growing into the water, uninhabited, I think. We got pine-apples here in perfection but not much other fruit. I am going ashore now to have a stroll before breakfast: (it is now only half-past six; so that I find I can tell you nothing more: and also that I have told you very little at all. Give my love to my father and all the Royal Family, not forgetting the Princess Royal and infants in the Terrace.

Tell Mary and Jane that if they come out here they would get husbands in a week. I shall write to James from Hong Kong. Believe me Dear Mother,

Your loving son

To his brother James
Wednesday, February 21st 1866

Instead of being angry that I have not written to you sooner, you ought to be flattered that I waited until I had time to send you a letter of respectable length. And first and foremost tell my mother (and make her mind easy) that I have discovered my spoons and forks in the sheep-skin trunk: *Hurray!* Let my father also tell Kelly that I have not a single article bought from him that can be depended upon. You know the tragic fate of the wooden box; the pig-skin burst at one corner, and had to be sewed by one of the sailors; and the sheep-skin has large patches of his hide torn off, exposing to view the paste board coats of his stomach. They will however do me as far as Peking. And now a word or two as to where I am. We left Sincapore last Wednesday, and had some rough weather shortly after leaving; but the motion of the ship was not much affected. We saw nothing remarkable on this run except a whale which was seen about a quarter of a mile from the vessel, blowing and lashing its tail about, as whales will do. We got into Hong Kong on Wednesday evening, after a seven days' trip. James Russell who went out to Hong Kong about four months ago from Belfast College had heard of our appointment and was down at the steamer accompanied by two other student interpreters to secure us at once, to stay with him while we were in port; which we did; and right well they entertained us. The races were going at Hong Kong, and we went to see them. As all races are pretty much alike I [shall] not describe them even to such a votary of the turf as yourself. Hong Kong is a very nice town indeed, sloping up from the sea to the middle of the hill called Victoria Peak. I believe by the way, that Victoria is the name of the town, and Hong Kong of the island. The weather was cool when I was there, but they tell me that in summer they have terrible heat. The town is so surrounded by hills that very little breeze can come at it. I saw another Belfast friend here, Jackson of the Bank of Ireland, who went from Ireland to Bombay and has since been transferred to Hong Kong. He was very glad to see me, and desired to be affectionately remembered to you and Johnny. Well, after spending a couple of very pleasant days there, we embarked on the P and O steamer *Ganges* for Shanghai. After we were a day out of port the weather was as cold as our winter, and the wind and sea frightfully rough. I have not seen such weather at all since leaving home: the waves absolutely swept clean over the whole quarter-deck. This lasted till within a day's run of Shanghai which we reached on Tuesday afternoon. [This must have been Tuesday the 27th of February J.S.P.] in the middle of torrents of rain. We landed our baggage and went straight to the Consulate. The Consul was in Hong Kong: but the *Vice* (Mr Markham) received us very kindly and recommended us to a Hotel where we are now. The government of course will pay all this. We go from Shanghai by steamer to Tientzin on the Peiho, and thence by carts overland to Peking, about 80 miles: the steamer leaves on Sunday morning so we have ample time to see all that can be seen, and that's not much. Shanghai is a very poor looking place indeed. The only respectable buildings in it are the Consulates, which are all on the south side of the river and pretty close together. The Chinese towns are very dirty—small houses, dirty lanes, and those very narrow; and the people are not a bit better nor worse than the other Chinese I have seen elsewhere. You are not to suppose that the Chinese is a coloured race. The prevailing complexion is of course yellow but they have a colour in their cheek, and some of them are as fair-skinned as English. The men are merry fellows, apparently; always laughing and in good humour; very tall strong fellows some of them are too. The women! the lovely women! They are decidedly better than I at all expected to find them. It is all humbug to think that they are all cripples with little feet. I have only seen two women with small feet since I came to China. They are little creatures and their feet are small enough, if let alone. They dress queerly enough. They wear a great-coat with pockets, of blue cloth and trousers of the same material but of a finer texture, boots like English women, and a coloured handkerchief over the head, or else no covering at all. An umbrella completes the picture, and you have a regular Shanghai belle. The pig-tails of the men reach to their heels, and end in a tassel of silk, woven or plaited in with the hair. To cut off a Chinaman's pig-tail is the most awful degradation with which you can punish him.

Until it grows again, none of his friends and relations speak to him or have any intercourse with him at all. None except such as are grandfathers are allowed to wear a moustache. The married women are known by their coiffure which consists of dressing up their hair at the back of the head somewhat like the handle of a tea-pot, the head being the pot and the nose the spout. In fact this style is called the tea-pot style. The men in the service here have shewn us a great deal of attention, and have had us to their houses. Today we went to one of them and had tiffin, Chinese fashion with chopsticks. They are made of ivory about a foot and a quarter long, coming to a point (not sharp however) to allow you to spear your morsels with them. They are both held in the right hand, and the object is to succeed in conveying the food between the points to your mouth; no very easy job I can tell you. The dishes are all cut small to allow you to lift one bit at a time. Finally, all eat out of the same dish. The chopsticks should not be put into the mouth, but the piece adroitly taken off them. To eat rice, you put the cup in which it is served, into your mouth, keeping the latter open and the rice is also lately shovelled in till your mouth is full, when you commence the process of mastication. What we call *grub* in English (?); they here call chów-chow (accented on the first).

Tell my mother that I called on Mr Marcel, Colonial Secretary of Hong Kong and now acting governor, and had a pleasant interview with him. I also called on Mr Walker, Mr Boyd's correspondent, who asked me to dinner and would have had me to stay, only [his] house was full at the time. He also placed his boat at my disposal to go to and from the steamer. All this was pleasant and I hope I made myself agreeable.

Now I have little or nothing left to add, except that there has been one continued downpour of rain ever since I came here. This would be distressing were there anything particular to do; but as there is not, I stay indoors and read, venturing out only on matters of necessity. The Vice-Consul told us that we must take with us an iron bed-stead, with mattress and blankets which are not provided by the Britannic Majesty's Government to poor students in their service. This will involve drawing some money from the Consulate here, which can be easily done. I shall buy a cheap iron bed, with hair mattress and a couple of pairs of blankets and towels and trust to fate for furnishing the rest of my apartments. All the men who have been at Peking are sorry to leave it. They say, one and all, "Enjoy yourself at Peking, for you will never have anything like it in any other part of China." Living there is so that they can live as comfortable on the £200 as they can in another place for £250 or £300. Every man is allowed home at the end of five years. This is certain, though most men who are waiting for promotion do not avail themselves of it for some time after.

I don't know how much they are allowed towards their passage home; not the whole of it at any rate. Parcels come out through the P and O Co. to men in the Government service, free four times a year. If my father would write to Mr Davidson he could tell him the terms of agreement with the Foreign Office on this subject. By the bye, if the parcel containing the odd pairs of boots has not been sent off before this arrives tell McCollum that the extra solid boot was torbitted [drawing] in this fashion. The inner lines represent the sewing merely and the middle one a line of ornamental holes punched. There was that angle in the middle that I have endeavoured to depict. The other was quite plain. It would be no harm to send me out another pair of extra solid boots also: for the ruffians stole my other strong pair entirely. If packed in a little deal case hooped with iron at both ends and fully directed, it cannot come to any harm. If you would put on the box *to be forwarded immediately*, my friends at Shanghai would do so much for me. Tell my mother then that I will send home whatever I can after getting the more necessary things I have mentioned. The currency here is Mexican dollars, each about the size, or nearly so, of a crown piece. Sovereigns only bring four dollars and a quarter; so there is no demand for them except by men going home who buy them at that price to carry them to England where they are gainers of $1/3$ on each sovereign. I unpacked my gun-case and found that the gun was perfectly safe and free from a speck of rust. I shall want it going from Tientsin to Peking, for as we go through unfrequented places, I may get a shot or two. The steamer that is to take us is the *Nantzing*, a paddle, and I believe very fast. Four days will take us to Tientsin and two or three more to Peking. I shall in due time let you know how I get on my way up. The cold will be going away by that time, and I shall not immediately want boots.

They tell me that there is a step-daughter of Sir Rutherford Alcock's at Peking, a Miss Lowder, who is very much admired, as being pretty, accomplished, lively, agreeable and withal only seventeen. All this inspires a hope that life at Peking may not be altogether disagreeable, or barbarian. I always think it the correct thing to wind up these accounts of myself and my doings by adding that I am well. I never was better than I am now, and the little run on shore will be of use to me, though if this horrid rain continues it must be very little running that I can do. And now, dearest fellow I have really and absolutely nothing more to say. My mother will of course see this, and you can tell my friends in the country what I am doing and how I have managed to do it hitherto. I shall write to Aunt Allen, and Aunt Eliza when I have a little more to tell them. At present one letter exhausts my ideas and experience alike. I am very comfortable in the hotel here; it is kept by an Englishman who does not serve up Chinese dishes, of which nobody but the cook can tell the composition. So now good bye, give my love to my Father, and my dear mother, and to all in College

1 Sir Rutherford Alcock, 1809–97, doctor turned diplomat, minister Japan 1859–65, China 1865–71.

Square and the Terrace. Andrew will like to hear how I am getting on, so you can let him know. Give him my love: and believe me, dear James,

Your loving brother

P.S.—The dates of this letter are incoherent. It was begun the day named above but was discontinued till today.   F.K.P.

Friday, March 2nd 1866—We got our passage tickets today for Tientsin, and start on Sunday morning. This is the first trip that has been made this year so far up the river, and we may possibly have to wait a few days before the ice will let us up. I was obliged to draw $60 today from the Vice-Consul to enable me to get a bed-stead and blankets: I am taking my chance of getting the rest of my bed-gear at Peking. I got a very good little bed-stead, plain, for $13 which was not dear, allowing for carriage from England. I could get no white blankets at all at Shanghai, and was obliged to buy red ones. This is my first exploit in housekeeping and I really do not much care if it was to be the last. The blankets are coarse but thick and warm. I shall manage to find out what the men at the Embassy do, and do likewise. Harvey is a good sort of fellow, if he had not such a good opinion of himself. He is however quite disposed to be useful and agreeable; and I think will turn out well when I know him longer. Whether he is in love or whether he is afflicted with some complaint that keeps him in a perpetual morbid silence I know not: but this I know that he does not speak more than a dozen words to any one in the course of a day, and mopes about.

I have now seen all of this place (Shanghai), that I can and am longing to get away from it. I should not care to live here at all, and the men tell me it is very expensive. My next letter will be from Peking, wherein I shall detail to you all the particulars relating to the arrival of the distinguished party at the capital of the Celestial Empire.

Your loving brother

To his Mother
British Legation, Peking—March 20th 1866

My last letter to James, brought me up to Shanghai. We left that place on the Sunday morning, following the day on which I wrote, for Tientsin on the Peiho, by the Steamer *Nan-zing*. We made the voyage in about four days; but on the morning of the 5th we ran upon the bar, and were kept there till a rise of the tide. Once inside the river's mouth, we saw nothing but ice; and after running up for seven miles we got blocked up and stopped. The ice further up the river had broken up; and floating down to the sea had got jammed closely together, to the depth of several feet in some places.—We waited there all that night, and half of the next day when a sudden crack in the ice set us free. A few hours after then brought us to Tientsin, where we arrived on Monday morning. We called on Mr Morgan the Consul, and found that carts had been provided for us, to start on the following morning; slept that night on board, and next day at about twelve o'clock set off for Peking. Mr Mitford, an attaché to the Legation, was going up at the same time, having come to Tientsin to bring back a box of dollars, as he knew all about the journey, and had his own cook with him, we were more comfortable than we could have been by ourselves.

And now for the far-famed carts. They are just large enough to hold one person besides the driver. They are covered over the top and up the sides and they have no springs: consequently when the mules were at full speed on a road the least of whose ruts was two feet deep, the unfortunate inmate was pounded into mummy, now flattening his skull against the roof of the vehicle,—anon rebounding from side to side, and never at rest for two minutes. Add to this that the dust blew in our faces in perfect clouds, and I think you will pity us! We took two nights and a day on the road, and arrived on Wednesday morning, no Thursday—at the wall of Peking. There was some little delay at the gate about passports and finally it was thrown open—and blinded and begrimed with dust—pounded into a sort of stupor by the jolting of the carts, with the populace getting round us, and for ought I know cursing us—the three unfortunate Student Interpreters rode into the capital of the Celestial Empire. The distance from the outer gate to the British Legation is six miles; and in our own drive thither we passed through the gate of the Tartar city in which the Legations all are. There are three cities that compose Peking. The most important is the Imperial City where is the palace of the Emperor, and into parts of which no European is permitted to enter. Surrounding it is the Tartar city, and on the outside is the Chinese city which is the largest of the three. They have each a wall entirely round them. The Chinese and the Imperial walls are not particularly large; but the Wall round the Tartar city is most stupendous. The top of it is at the narrowest parts twenty five yards or paces wide; and where there is a buttress, I stepped fifty long paces. The surface is paved with solid stone cubes, a foot every

1 'An-tin Mun, the gate of Pekin in our possession—from a sketch
by our special artist': *Illustrated London News*, 5 January 1861

way, and the walls are built of bricks, quite as hard as any stone. The
masonry is perfect. It is about eighty feet high. Well, we got to the
Legation about two in the afternoon and saw most of the men that day
and had our rooms allotted to us. The luggage being drawn by bullocks
came a day late. I have been obliged to get a lot of furniture for my
room, for I found that I was turned into an apartment whose chief
ornaments were four bare walls and a stove. The articles I purchased
are however of the commonest description and the amount will not
break me. Pay day does not come round till the 1st of April, and the
furniture has been got by the Legation, the amount to be stopped out
of my first instalment. I shall be able to send you home something but
you see we did not calculate on *furnishing*; and that is a tolerable item
at first. The next day I put on a respectable rig out, and called on Sir
Rutherford Alcock, and saw him and Miss Lowder. He was very
gracious and invited us to Lady Alcock's reception which takes place
every Friday night and to which all the Europeans in Peking repair—
Russians, Prussians and French. I also dine there tomorrow night. Lady
Alcock has been ill for some time and I have not seen her. The daughter
is good looking but without any expression. There is a brother of hers
who has been nine years in the navy and goodness knows where else

besides; but when the mother was married to the English Minister, he was brought to the Legation and loafs about, doing nothing.

· The buildings now occupied by the British Legation were formerly the palace of a prince of the royal dynasty who let the place to the English.[1] There are in it six or seven disjointed blocks of buildings scattered all over it, and the whole is surrounded by a wall. Our rooms are in a row of two-storey houses set apart for the students alone and we do what we like and no one meddles with us. Mr Wade[2] has set us some work to do, and gives us each a Chinese teacher who comes to our rooms whenever sent for. The Assistant Chinese Secretary is John McLeavy Brown,[3] a man from the Queen's College Belfast. He is allowed to be the best Chinese speaker (among the English) in China; and has got a very nice post here where living is cheaper than at the ports. There are four other students: O'Brien from Cork, McClatchey from Dublin and two Scotchmen. There is thus not an Englishmen in our mess at all. We have a large room for our own mess and everything is provided; spoons, forks and napkins. For our share in the mess utensils, we pay an entrance fee of $.55 each. What the quarterly subscription for chow-chow is I don't yet know. We have a capital cook, and the table is well supplied with everything. Those who want beer and wine supply it for themselves from Tientsin. Neither commodity is much used here. We get abundance of wild fowl, and latterly we have been having a kind of wild venison from Mongolia, which is most delicious. Grapes we have all the year round.

The weather is very fine now, cold in the mornings, but quite warm and bright in the middle of the day. The last two students, who came up in the month of October have not yet seen a drop of rain. The chief draw-back is the dust which is consequent upon such continued drought. Most of the men here keep ponies which they buy from the Tartars, who bring them down from the hills; 20 dollars is about the usual price. They are small but very strong and very fast. The only place where a pedestrian can enjoy any comfortable exercise here is on the wall. The filth and stench of the streets are most abominable and render walking in them quite impossible. The city is full of fine old trees, and looking from the walls the whole city round about seems

---

1 Incorrect: Alcock did ask for a royal palace but his request was turned down and he had to rent one belonging to a nobleman.

2 Sir Thomas Wade, 1818–95, Cambridge graduate, army, interpreter Hong Kong 1843, Chinese secretary Hong Kong 1855, Peking 1861–71, minister to China 1871–83, professor of Chinese, Cambridge 1888.

3 John McLeavy Brown became chief commissioner of Korean customs 1893–1913.

more like a forest than an inhabited town. Whereas in the south of China the women do not largely [go] into diminishing the feet, in Peking every woman is a cripple. Ages have passed since I feasted my eyes on a good dog; the curs of China are more like hungry wolves than dogs. One needs to carry either a stick or a whip to keep them off at times, for they lie in wait and dart at your legs from behind. They are thorough cowards; and I have often wished for some of our terriers to shake them out of their skin. But that cannot be.

And now dear Mother, that all the bustle and excitement of travelling are over, will you wonder, if for the first time since I was a week away from you all, I feel a little homesick? Everything here is so different from anything at home that I sometimes wonder what I should have replied to any one who one year ago had told me that I should be among a strange people and conforming to foreign customs within twelve revolutions of the moon. I have sometimes wakened in the early morning and started when I began to reflect that I was in Peking and not in College Square. But you are not to imagine from this that I am melancholy or desponding. Far from either. But I cannot help when by myself, letting my thoughts dwell upon *home* more frequently than on anything else. Then however comes the reflection that I am earning my own bread, and am never again to be burdensome to anyone; and that the harder I work the sooner I am likely to see you all again. Whether I can put by a little money or not, in the meantime I am supporting myself, and that's a good thing. When I am fairly fixed in my quarters (for I have still some things to get) I shall sit down and write to Bella and to as many of the rest as I shall manage to write to.

I hope dear Andrew has by this time got over his illness and has recovered his strength. Tell him that I should like to have a copy of the first likeness he gets done with his new beard. I think I asked you for one or two of myself done off the large picture. I have to send a couple to Manilla, to the Spanish admiral and his lieutenant who, I told you, came with me from Gibraltar to Hong Kong. The mailbag leaves Peking about once a fortnight, and you may depend on a line from me every Mail. I am looking anxiously for the *first* letter from home. The Mail is expected in at the end of this week and if you wrote by the first Mail after my departure, I shall have it by that arrival. Tell Johnny and James to drop me a line, no matter how short whenever they have time and I will answer them they may reckon on it. As I shall be writing once a fortnight, I can from time to time be giving you a little Chinese news, as I make acquaintance with Chinese manners and customs. By the way I want my card struck off and about 500 copies struck off and sent to me, for there is so much calling to be done here, that I am sadly at a loss. New comers are expected to visit every old resident, and I have already called at the Prussian and Russian Legations where by dint of French I made myself understood. The best form for the card is I suppose "Mr Francis K. Porter", with no address whatever, I can add that in pencil from time to time, as I may be different places.

And now to conclude and finish, I am in excellent health, never was better in all my life. When I left the last ship I weighed 9st 9lbs, shewing an increase of 3 lb since I left "the ould counthry". My luggage arrived perfectly safe.

Give my love to my father, to Bella, and Sandy, Andrew and the boys, not forgetting Maggie and my dear friends in Green Island, and, believe me, Dearest Mother, Ever your loving son

March 25th 1866—I find that I have still a few things that will interest you, and I accordingly open up the letter.

I have now got all I want for my room (for I have only one) and am hard at work with the language. My *sien-shang* (teacher) is a little dried up old fellow, but one of the most perfect gentlemen I ever saw. He comes to me for two hours and a half before breakfast, which is at the fashionable hour of 12½ p.m. and as long afterwards as I choose to keep him, I generally put on the tea-pot and give him a good cup; and you should see us both hobnobbing with cups of tea instead of glasses of sherry. He is in the most capital good humour then; but on the days when no tea is produced I find the work some way or other gets on slower. Tell my father that I am at present engaged in learning up the 214 radicals, which must be thoroughly mastered first of all. I find little difficulty in the pronunciation and I don't see why a man can't learn the form of a character in time, but the others are very mischief. There are in the Peking dialect four tones, and the same word, pronounced with those four voice inflections has a different meaning each time: and to remember the tone of the word according to the meaning you wish to represent, is, you may imagine, a little difficult for a young hand. I am doing about six nouns a day with the teacher, and occasionally an hour or two more by myself, and I think that is enough till I know enough of the language to read a book or two.

I dined yesterday at Sir Rutherford Alcock's and sat down to a very swell dinner. He has a French chef, who turns out a first rate entertainment. Two of the foreign ministers were there for dinner, and in the evening about thirty more gentlemen arrived. Lady Alcock is still confined to her room by a cold.

2 'Curiosity-Street, Pekin—from a sketch by our special correspondent':
Illustrated London News, 16 February 1861

We have a very nice little church in the Legation grounds, regularly fitted as an English place of worship. A.W. Collins is chaplain to the Legation and performs the services. There are ever so many missionaries here, or as they are familiarly termed "devil-dodgers", a highly irreverent title. I have called on some of them already and find them agreeable enough. On the whole I may say that I like the place and the people about me very well though they both are strangers to me. McKean and I have one house to ourselves: that's to say we have each one room on the top (or second) storey, and a bath-room down stairs, [and] a room each, for the boys and the coolie. We each keep a boy to whom we pay $6 a month: the coolie is between us, and costs $4. One man could [do] more than the work for both; but they won't and the coolie performs such menial offices as lighting the fires, cleaning boots and keeping the baths always full. The boys are most perfectly honest. They bring back every cent of change when sent on errands, and my things do not appear to be diminishing. If I caught him stealing I should lick him well, and have him expelled the Legation: for it is a great privilege for boys to be allowed into the Legation even to apply for situations.

The races come on the 4th of April, and every one who has a pony rides a race. There will be about 40 animals altogether and the whole place is in excitement about the approaching event.

The tea I get here is not good. They put some strong scent into it, which also gives it a bitter taste. There are however several varieties but none of them palatable to me, except that intended for export to England. I may in time come to like it.

I find that although this letter has reached a good length, it contains singularly little news. You must excuse this. I am a bad bad letter writer. Love to all again: and to yourself. Believe me dear Mother, your loving son

Dear Mother—Forgive the disjointed way in which this letter has been written. I should not have perplexed you by any further addition to its already preposterous length, but that after coming in today from a six mile walk upon the wall, after church, I found a letter and two papers lying on my table addressed in a well-known hand. As the first news from home for three months, you may imagine I hailed them with joy. Your news and that of Andrew especially is very gratifying . No less so are the good wishes towards me expressed by my father yourself and my two brothers.

As regards Willie I am not in a position to say what the chances of success are of coming out to China in a mercantile line. In Peking there is no European business whatever except that of the Legation and customs so of course as far as I am concerned he might as well be in Port Elizabeth as in Hong Kong, for I should not see him at all. But with good recommendations, he ought, I think to get a good situation in Hong Kong within a bank or in the customs, or even in a large mercantile house of which the largest in China are there. But I think he should be very cautious on coming *on chance*. Of this however, he and my father are of course better judges than I. If he ever comes up Peking way, there is a bed for him, and a dollar or two in the bag if he wants them. I hope however that you will see him at home first; for a quiet talk with you would soon effect an arrangement that would be satisfactory. I shall write to himself before another Mail goes out, but shall not mention his proposed movements. I intend also to write to Uncle William. Poor Maggie! and is her toe as bad as ever? Tell her that the only objection to amputation of the afflicted member, is that the other one must come off, to enable her to keep her equilibrium! I doubt if ever her (hitherto) indomitable courage is equal to that!

To return to myself: I am working at the language as hard as I can. The weather still necessitates a fire in my room by day, and I make myself pretty comfortable during my studies. As I am to be located in this quiet out of the way place for two whole years, I have determined to study more than Chinese alone; and (as one cannot spend more than a certain time every day at it, and there is still some to spare) I propose to go on with my old studies of Greek and Latin, and I think Hebrew. Of course I cannot occupy more than two or three hours a day with this extra duty; but even with that I can learn a little in two years. If my father would write me out a few directions, such as he prepared for me when I commenced the language and which are not contained in a simple form in any grammar, I can perhaps get a Gesenius,[1] a dictionary and a Bible at some of the posts. I was sorry to read the account of Mr McAlester's[2] failure in the professorate. The opposition seem to have shewn their usual "love of concord", and their usual vituperation. I was glad to observe that my father snubbed that slimy hypocrite Jellie.[3] The paper contained little interesting matter besides that: and indeed we have a good reading room that receives the principal papers

1 Heinrich Frederick Wilhelm Gesenius, 1786–1842, Hebrew philologist, author of two lexicons.
2 Charles J. McAlester delivered the address in John Scott Porter's church on 8 July 1880 on the occasion of Porter's death.
3 Revd John Jellie, Unitarian minister, York Street, Belfast.

and magazines of the home circuit. There is a good library also; so I am not lost for want of reading; but I am always right glad to hear home news, and a local paper now and then will always be acceptable.

I must now positively and really close up this letter, or else you will not in future [want] more than half of one so long. With love again to all, believe me, dearest mother

Your loving son,

To his Mother
British Legation, Peking—April 11th, 1866

I fear that this Mail must go out without bringing you anything that can be called news. No Mail has arrived since the departure of my last letter, and I therefore have no letters to reply to: but I can at least tell you that I am alive and passing my days, pleasantly and quietly. The temporary excitement of the races has produced a proportionate depression and things are now once again going on in their old routine. For the sake of my sporting brothers I may state that the races were completely successful, and that the running of the ponies was by no means contemptible. The ground was given to the race Committee by a rich old Chinaman, and a very handsome present it is. It is about four miles from the Legation, and we ride to it through the bed of the Grand Canal which is now quite dry. The only incident that occurred to mar the harmony of the day was that the Chinese mob pelted the pony phaëton with Miss Lowder in it as it was leaving the ground. Fortunately no one was struck except one of the escort; and Mr Murray, the Accountant of the Legation, and private secretary of Sir Rutherford, put himself at the head of the men, and charged them; he cutting them with the but end of his hunting whip, and the men laying about them with the flat of their swords. The dastards of course fled in dismay. The circumstance, though in itself comparatively trifling served to show the disposition of the lower people to the "foreign devils" as we are elegantly termed. I have not many opportunities of getting an insight into the private and domestic life of the Chinese but when I can speak a little Murray and Brown will take me with them when they go to visit some of the old fellows whom they know, and I shall tell you all I see. They certainly are, as a nation, the most polite people I ever saw. I have seen two coolies meeting one another in the court-yard and bowing to each other with a really well-bred air. My little teacher carries his politeness to such an extent that he leaves the room always to blow his nose!

And now a few words about the obscure individual who pens this document. I am getting by degrees a number of gaudy Chinese pictures to take off the dead bareness of the walls of my apartment; but if you should at any time see anything in any of the illustrated papers that would answer the same end you would confer a great blessing on your perplexed offspring by sending it to me. I have got my pony but have not yet got my furniture or mess bills, so I do not [know] what I am to pay away. The only coin here is the Mexican dollar; but there are bank notes, issued of course, by the Chinese for certain numbers of *tiaos* a sum worth 7¹/₂d. These are convenient for dealing with the Chinese, but for all else are useless. I forgot to say that there are brass coins, called *cash* about the size of a half penny, round with a square hole punched in the centre; but these are only used for paying coolies for jobs, or such like. There are upwards of 4000 of them in a dollar. When I can get an opportunity of sending home a small box of *spacements* I will put in some of all these curiosities. To revert to myself. I am in robust health. The weather now is perfectly heavenly and if it were not for the dirty streets and roads life would be almost too enjoyable. I very often get a mount from some of the men who keep two horses and I can now ride with both ease and comfort, not to speak of a certain amount of elegance. We are all going off to the hills in the summer time to avoid the heat and perfumes of the city; but of this more, when more is arranged. Easter passed with little vivacity. I hope you enjoyed it more at home. Give my love to my father, and to all in College Square and to Murray's Terrace, and remember me to Mary and Jane. Probably next Mail will bring more news from

    Your loving son

To his Mother
British Legation, Peking—April 25th 1866

Your welcome letters came safely to hand by the last Mail, and I was delighted to see that the boys have not yet begun to tire of writing to me. Your news was just exactly of the kind that most interests me, local events that occur in your own sphere. My father is going to send me a summary of my outfit, which he says is heavy. What I can contribute I shall willingly send: I can't of course clear it off in a day; but remittances from time to time will always be of some use. I have written to Bella by this Mail. I hope she will find the news readable. And poor Polly! I shall write to her by next Mail. I am waiting for a supply of stamps before I can write Billy or my Uncle William. And now for a few words about my humble self.

I am studying my appointed time without interruption, and I find that there is no impossibility about mastering the language. It is all through a matter of mere memory, both as regards the (written) character and the sound. My teacher tells me that my ear is very correct, and my pronunciation good, and that is one step. But in the meantime I am not neglecting the body altogether. I have either a walk or a ride every day, and we have a gymnasium where we exercise in the morning at about seven o'clock; and a cold sponge bath completes the process. On Saturday last I rode out with Murray, the accountant and private Secretary, to Sir Rutherford's temple, which he has taken for the summer but has not yet occupied, so we had the whole place to ourselves.

We sent our bedding out by a cart and took our boys to cook. We stayed there all Sunday and came in on Monday morning. It was almost the only breath of fresh air that I have had since I came; for at this season the dust is flying and covering everything. On our way home, we passed a place called Yuen-Ming-Yuen—a summer temple or place of the Emperor which was sacked and fired by Lord Elgin some six years ago. You recollect probably the account of the fearful wanton havoc made by our soldiers among the costly ornaments and furniture. I am going through it next week and shall then give you an account of it. The present dynasty is Tartar: *Ching* I think is the name of it. The last was the *Ming*, Chinese. In the fall of the year I am going up on an excursion into Mongolia and I shall then see the Ming tombs. They are remarkable as being the only tombs in existence of a previous dynasty, for when a new dynasty comes in it smashes at once the tombs of its predecessors: so they are doubly curious on this account.

The weather is now very warm and the trees have come out all at once. If it were not for the dust, it would be delicious; even as it is, it is endurable. Everything goes on in the same way: no change from day to day except when an occasional little trip like the one above, relieves the monotony. I still continue to enjoy the very best health and by dint of my gymnastic exercises I soon hope to have no contemptible amount of strength. I think that I am still growing a little, but of course very little. I am naturally anxious to hear how James is getting on in that

3 'A portion of the Emperor of China's summer palace, near Pekin':
Illustrated London News, 27 April 1861

line. I suppose the boys have begun their cricketing again. We cannot have the game here, for there is not a blade of grass. I was very much delighted to hear that Andrew is so much better; I hope he is by this time quite well again. Give him my dear love. And now, my darling mother, I have told you all I can. As I see more of the people and the place I shall have more interesting matter to tell you ; for the present however, good bye. Give my best love to my father and the boys; and with the same to yourself, believe me

Ever your loving son

To his Father

British Legation, Peking—May 8th 1866

My letter to my mother merely contains the information that I am alive
and kicking without going into details; and I think I can add a little
more than that to the home budget.

As you are no doubt anxious to hear the system I pursue in learning
the language, I shall tell you. Mr Wade who is the Chinese Secretary
and Chief Secretary of the Legation is the chief overseer of the
students. He has compiled a series of exercises, not yet published,
though ready for publication, of which we all have manuscript copies.
The exercises contain a vocabulary with all the sounds of the characters
used in each, and the tone of the character marked by number, and the
English meaning. Then the words are arranged in sentences which we
read over with the teacher till we can read the characters fluently,
applying the proper tones. Besides this, I am getting up a speaking
vocabulary of my own, by asking the teacher, (who cannot speak a
word of English), the names of different objects, and different ways of
expressing the same idea; so I am not wasting my time. I also write
each character as I go along, to impress the form upon my memory.
Some men have a better eye for the character and others a better ear
for sound. I find I am of the latter class; for I frequently forget the form
of the character altogether, when by hearing the sound I can tell the
meaning at once.

As I mentioned to my mother in my last letter, I am going up into
Mongolia for a tour this autumn, Sir Rutherford willing. All the men
whom I have met who were there, describe it as a most enjoyable trip.
We send on mule carts, a day or two before with directions at what
towns or villages to stop and we follow, on mules or ponies.

The Ming tombs I have set my heart on seeing. The present dynasty
is the *Taching*: *ta* being *great*, and *ching, purse* (probably their predecessors were "the great unwashed"). On all porcelain of any value, the
name or the seal of the dynasty or reign when it was made is marked;
on it collectors of antique specimens rely as to the age. I have seen
some exquisite porcelain, of all shapes and the most perfect colours;
the specimens are however dear: but I hope to be able to send you some
which, though not the dearest or best that can be got, will still show
you what the Chinese can do in colouring. Meantime I am not making
much progress in the "construction of a fortune". But I hope to be able
to send home before long what will go a good way toward paying for

my outfit—I should have written both to Willie and my Uncle William, if I could have procured stamps but there are none to be had. There is a supply however, coming up from Hong Kong in a few days and I shall then write to them.

I have written to my mother what I know about the Chinese Customs. From what has come under my own observation it is an infinitely better service than mine—though [there] is a chance (a very remote one) that the Chinese may on any caprice, get rid of all their foreign servants; especially as they are now educating the Mandarin's sons to a very large extent to learn English. Two or three sons of Chinese officials have lately gone home to England, along with Mr Hart, probably for the purpose of studying the language there. Then the question is, would Willie, supposing he got into the service, (there is no examination, but direct appointment from Mr Hart)—would he care to begin to grind and study such a language, after having all his life worked at a wholly different employment.

As I see more of the city and country about here, I shall let you know what I think of it, Believe me dear Father

Your loving son

P.S.—Sir Rutherford Alcock is at present reading your *Principles of Textual Criticism*. I am anxious to have his opinion of it.

To his Mother

British Legation, Peking—May 8th, 1866

I have received the last two Mails without having an opportunity of sending off an answer to them as yet. The arrival is much more punctual than the departure; and if any Mail reaches England without a letter from me, you may know that it brought no Mail from Peking. I had intended to write to you a much longer letter: but for the last three nights I have not been in bed. Murray of whom you have heard, (or rather *seen*) me speak, got a severe fall from his horse on Saturday, as we were all going to the temple in the hills. Sir Rutherford, who is by profession a surgeon, not a diplomatist, attended to his wound (on the head) and we took it in turns, to sit up day and night to watch him, and to put cold cloths on his head to keep down brain fever which was apprehended. He is now quite better and able to go about a little.

I am still dodging away in the same old track and have not seen anything new since I wrote to you last. The last few days have been cooler and today there is an even downpour of rain—a luxury here. If it clears up in the afternoon, walking in the city will be practicable.

By the way, if you could manage to get Willie into the Customs here, it would be about the best thing he could do; except that he would perhaps not care to study at the language like a school-boy at his time of life. There is no limit of age: but of course young fellows are preferable, as being likely to be longer of active use to the service. They all begin as student interpreters with a salary of £400; just double mine! and their promotion is both speedier and better paid. They are, of course, entirely under the Chinese Government; and Hart, who is now gone home, has the power, and I believe the sole power, of taking men into the service. I know all the Customs men here, and what I tell you is exactly what they tell me, and I have every reason to think it correct. Hart himself left the Consular service, to take service under the Chinese.

I see by the Shanghai papers that Mr Dow, to whom I had Mr Boyd's introduction, has sued for and obtained a divorce from his wife.

You will, long before this, have received my note, saying that the spoons arrived all right. They were exactly in the position you described, and I am very glad to have them now.

I don't [know] that I mentioned in my last letter, that we had taken a temple for the summer months. The arrangement about payment is deferred till we leave the place, and then a present of a small sum of money is given to the head priest. There is a large hall in our temple containing five hundred images of the mighty Buddha, in different positions.

I am picking up a few little things occasionally that would be curiosities at home but are common here; and I mean before leaving Peking to send you home a box of them. The best articles all come from Canton where the artificers are much more skilful than here, though some of the old China here is really beautiful. Mitford, one of the attachés, is employed by one of the Rothschilds to collect *curios* for him. He has already collected about £1000 worth, chiefly China-ware, and carved crystals.

I intended also by this Mail to write to the friends in the country, particularly to Aunt Allen and Miss Knowles;[1] but really I cannot do

1 Aunt Allen, a courtesy aunt, was the wife of W.J.C. Allen of Greenisland; Miss F. Knowles conducted a Select Day School at 30 Upper Arthur Street between the 1830s and the 1850s; she is the source of Porter's second Christian name.

so. There is a better time coming. Many thanks for Maggie's letters. She is evidently enjoying herself much. Give my love to all friends, and to all at home and in Murray's Terrace: and believe me, Dear Mother,

Your loving son

P.S.—You will be glad to hear that my whiskers are now a reality. "This was sometime a paradox: but now the time gives it proof"!

Tell my father that the *Whig* has come out all right as yet—Many thanks for it. You did *not* write an answer to mine from Aden. Tell Andrew that I am reserving myself for a long letter to him—F.K.P.

To his Mother

British Legation, Peking—May 26th 1866

I have delayed beginning my letter to you till the last minute in hope that the home Mail, due here today would arrive in time for me to answer, or at least to say that I had received your letters.

Something however must have detained it, for we have heard of its arrival at Shanghai, and as yet it has not come to the fore. I have less news this fortnight to relate than on any former occasion, chiefly because I have been in the Legation walls almost the whole time, and there is not much exciting matter going on there. Sir Rutherford and his household have removed to the temple in the hills: and we have taken a temple and at present there are two of our men out, looking after the repairing of roofs, and sweeping out of rooms, I expect to join them on Monday next. I am afraid that we are going out too soon; for the violent heat and no less violent mosquitos have not yet come forth in full vigour, and we should enjoy the temple much *then*. We must however stay there the longer. The last fortnight has been perfectly heavenly. We have had very severe rain, almost every night and morning, and the day is so cool and fresh after it. The corn in the fields is all in ear, and will soon be ready for cutting: after which the same fields will produce a second, sometimes a third crop. The potatoes here are excellent; quite as good as those at home; but the cooks have not the same skill in boiling them. The only day that I was out of the Legation since I wrote to you, was last Monday when I went up one of the hills to the Northwest of the city. The day was quite clear, and I saw upwards of thirty miles all round. With the help of the field-glasses, I saw the place where the Ming tombs are, and the walled city of Chan-ping-chow; called by some "Jumping Joe"—the two sounds are so much alike that if you ask a Chinaman the way to Jumping Joe he does not perceive the difference and tells you [as if you] had said Chan-ping-chow. There is a river to the west of the city which flows into the Peiho, about 30 miles south of Peking, called the Hwin-Ho (the muddy river) over which there are several marble bridges of large size. Peking is thus in a plain with a considerable river on each side of it. There all kinds of fruits produced, and each season has its fair share; so that even in winter there is fresh fruit of some kind. You will perceive that I give a few more particulars of its environs in every letter, and by the time I leave Peking, you may be able to form some idea of what it is: you must own that I am so bad a describer that it will take you at least that time to form one!

And now for some questions about home. Is there any further news about Willy? You must be very anxious to hear from him about his movements, and I can assure you that I am very eager for the latest news about him. Since I last wrote to you (when you will recollect I mentioned the Customs service in China as a good thing for Willy), I have been thinking that the same thing would apply to James. I think it is a terrible pity that a fellow like him should now be growing up into a man, with such a small prospect as he has. My salary is small enough here; but still better than his at home; and if he could be got into the Customs, he would start on £400 and have allowances as to quarters, furniture and other things, that we here never get. The building in which the Customs business is carried on in Peking is at present being knocked down to make more accommodation for an increased number of hands. The young hands are almost all sent to Peking, to learn the Mandarin, the official language, and it is thought that Hart[1] will give some nominations (that is direct appointments) to the Queen's College Belfast, and to some of his fellow townsmen. Think over it and let me know if you do anything in the matter. You don't know the comfort it would be to me, if I had one of my brothers here with me. As regards promotion the service is immeasurably before ours.

I had thought to write to Andrew by this Mail, and to Maggie: but I am sorry I must [put] it off till next Mail. I am quite well myself, and am getting on at the language with as much speed as I can make.

1 Sir Robert Hart, 1838–1911, BA Queen's University in Ireland, 1853, MA 1871, hon. LLD 1882, inspector general of Chinese maritime customs 1863–1906.

4 Tombs of the Emperors of the Ming dynasty at Nankin:
Illustrated London News, 18 February 1861

The French cook took smallpox in the Legation some three weeks ago; and as it was so near us, I got vaccinated with success. The man is well again and no one has taken the disease. The medical man of the Legation is Dr Dudgeon of Ayr in Scotland; a young man, and apparently a skilful fellow; he is also a kind of missionary and draws about £300 a year more for that, and is consequently well enough off.

I think I forgot to tell you the last time I wrote that I get the *Whig* regularly. Many many thanks for it! In another month's time I hope to be able to send you home some money. I hope you will be staying somewhere at the shore this year. I think it always does you an immensity of good. I always derived benefit from it *in my weak state of health*!

The Mail box closes tonight, and I shall not be able to mention the arrival of your letters, unless the Mail comes in before 5 o'clock this afternoon. Give my love to my father and brothers, to all in the Terrace, to all in Green island, and to the Sherrards in Gusset-hall. Remember me also to Mary and Jane, those two paragons of female virtue: and believe me my dear Mother,

Sunday May 27th—My dear Mother, The departure of the Mail has been delayed one day, and now the home Mail has just come in, I have only half an hour to compose. Many thanks for your letter and thank

James and Johnny for theirs. I also got a charming letter from Polly. Tell them that without fail I shall write to them all three, and to Andrew by next fortnight. You mention having sent the *Weekly Whig*: none has arrived by this Mail, nor has the paper that Johnny mentions having sent. If you send me a *Christian Unitarian*, it also has been stopped. I am greatly disappointed at not getting the account of the Graduates' Deputation; and the Delacherois–Tennent trial,[1] which you mention as having been fully reported.

This Mail is late; and there is another now due at Shanghai, whence it should come to us in seven days. A courier runs with the bags from Tientsin across country to Peking, travelling day and night and arrives within the 30 hours. My papers have have been held over till next Mail. I am sorry that my father has had another tussle with his old enemy [*lumbago*], but he has escaped it appears with a tolerably easy victory. Andrew's convalescence is also delightful news: (no not *also*) I shall be in the Legation the whole of next fortnight with only one companion, and I shall have time to write the promised letters. I had intended going to the hills among the first; but the present weather is so cool here that I am inclined to stay in the city now, to escape the hot months. Love again to all,

Your ever loving son

To his Mother

HBM Legation, Peking—May 31st 1866

"It was a summer's evening—Old Gaspar's work was done"—and he was sitting at his open window sipping bohea—"his custom always of an afternoon," when the sound most dear, of all others here, "the Mail is in" came, wafted on the breeze. I had not expected it for a fortnight after the arrival of the last, and here it was within a week after it. No one but one who has lived at a distance from home and has had all day plenty of work to occupy him, can imagine the delight and satisfaction of sitting down to read home letters. Thanks to you all, I have a plentiful stock of letters to read over, every Mail; more than can be said of all the men here.

---

1 A sensational trial reported in the *Northern Whig* of 11 March 1866 of Robert James Tennent, a prominent Belfast gentleman, for a vicious assault on Nicholas Delacherois of Donaghadee for the alleged maltreatment of his wife, Tennent's sister. Tennent was sentenced to twelve months' imprisonment.

5 'Peking cab': *Illustrated London News*, 23 February 1861

I am glad that my Galle letter, of whose existence you had given up hope, has arrived. I recalled what a wretched patched up scrawl it was; but still it shewed you that I was well; and up to the date of my arrival in Ceylon had not forgotten you.

The chief news of your letters, is of course that of Johnnie's new appointment. It is very delightful that his services have been so well recompensed; and never did man deserve a rise more than he did. Coming so soon after my departure, his will of course be deplored greatly by you all; and I hope that his settling there may be an additional inducement for you and my father to take a holiday trip across the Channel. I shall write and congratulate him by this Mail. Before this letter can reach you, he will be settled in his new quarters. It is one comfort that he has some warm friends where he is going who will make his isolation more endurable. And now poor old James is left all by himself! How little did we three brothers, who sat at the same table and slept in the same room, and never were two months separated from one another in our lives, think that three or four months would roll round and find one of the trio in London, and the most worthless of them in the capital of the Chinese empire. Drummond is however growing up, and will soon be a companion for him, and another year will see the dear little sister home from school, I suppose; and before that he will have become reconciled to his *solitude*. After this news of Johnnie's new settlement, of course what I referred to in my last, as applicable and suitable for James will be at once discarded.

Willy's continued silence is both distressing and mysterious. I make no doubt however that if next Mail bring no letter from him, it will be because he is on his way home to you. I am confirmed in this by Mr Conway's impression that, lacking funds, he would work his passage home. If he should come home and settle to go out again to China, let him be cautious of coming out on the chance of an appointment. From what I hear that is in every way an unprofitable speculation. Living at any port in China is excessively dear, and if he were any time without obtaining a situation, he would find himself in a very deplorable case. But you and my father will no doubt have settled that in your own heads before you allow him to take any definite step. I have not yet been able to procure stamps, or I should have written to him long ago.

I am very very glad to find that my father's attack of "rheumatiz" has been only temporary; as Mr Barnett used to say of a tooth of mine which he was manoeuvering to get out: and which in nine cases out of ten would have stayed in my head till I was a grey-headed man. I know of old what time of his is taken up by visiting, and don't expect him to write more than once in three months. By the way, you talk of Janet's baby without ever previously informing me that such an event had taken place. Some of your letters mentioned that a similar event was expected from Mrs Nixon Porter: let me know when it takes place. I am always glad to hear of relations and friends; and I am by the way very glad to hear that I am not yet forgotten by some of the latter, as my father mentioned to me that he had been asked about me tolerably often. I see by the papers the marriage of our cousin Tony Porter to Mr Plunkett. Had her mother abandoned her bed to which she took on hearing the fatal news, before her daughter's nuptials? And did the father drink a stirrup-cup out of the Communion chalice? Johnnie mentions that Aunt Finlay is positively coming home this year. I am afraid that her absence has been more desired than her return. Time will tell.

For myself I am getting along well. Study of the language is progressing. I have not much amusement except what I derive from sauntering through the city, and in order to do so, it is necessary to leave at home all your sense of smell or to make use of that sense as little as you can. I saw the other evening a very gorgeous wedding procession, bringing home the bride of some Chinese swell. She was in a palanquin—a splendid one, sparking with polished metal and gilding; and about 200 attendants on foot accompanied her, carrying each a lantern and beating gongs. I had seen several before, but none equal to this.

From the wall at this season the Tartar city is like one vast wood, with here and there a roof peeping out, and a column of smoke curling up through the trees. The only roofs distinctly seen are the yellow tiles of the imperial palace buildings. The imperial colour is a *dirty yellow*; and it is a strange fact that throughout the length and breadth of this, the largest empire in the world, no subject from the highest mandarin to the beggar dares to have a roof to his house of the same colour. I have seen several Chinaware articles such as cups and saucers, vases and other things that were taken when the palace at Yuen-Ming-Yuen[1] was sacked by our troops, and the groundwork of them is of the same yellow colour. Whether all the royal tea and dinner services are of the same ground colour, I cannot say. Near the palace is an artificial hill, built of coal or anthracite and grown over with trees.[2] There is a summer residence on it where the last emperor of the Ming dynasty,[3] committed suicide, having previously killed his "empresses" when the Tartars took his capital and sacked his palace.

But I have wandered away from my subject. You ask me if I am comfortable—I am indeed: and have every reason to be satisfied that I am *so* comfortable. I find it inconvenient enough to have no more than one room at my disposal; but I hope that before winter I shall have another one. The rooms downstairs, at present occupied by the servants and the baths are to be converted into sitting rooms, one for each man, and new premises will be built in the rear for the "boys".

By the way I had almost forgotten to tell you that the last two Mails brought me *no Whigs*. I am afraid that the Foreign Office officials don't care to encumber the bag with papers. It would be better to put 2d on each of them, and I am then sure of getting them. Brown gets Belfast papers, the *Newsletter*; and he and I exchange papers; so it was through his that I got my local news. I read the Delacherois–Tennent affair; and agree with you that the lady was drunk on the occasion referred to in court. Still my sympathies go with Tennent: for I think if I was told on all hands that a sister of mine was being ill-treated, so that I could not help taking notice of it, I should serve the offender out in something of the same way.

I shall be anxious to hear the agreement you came to about letting the old house. I doubt if in Belfast you will get another that will suit you as well; but your family is now smaller than it was; and if you can

---

1 The Summer Palace burnt by the British and French in 1860.
2 Coal Hill, probably so called becasue coal was piled there during the building of the palace.
3 Zhong Zhen.

hit on one with a room large enough for the books, that's all you want.—And now I have fairly run to the end of my tether and must bring this to a close. Rambling and disjointed as it is, I know it will be pleasant to *you*, my dearest mother. Give my dear love to my Father and brothers, and to all in the Terrace. I write to Maggie by this Mail, so bye, bye. I am ever your loving son

Friday, June 5th—Last night as I was leaving the Map-room I missed the stone from my ring: but on looking for it, found it on the floor where I had been sitting. They tell me there is no one in Peking who could mend it neatly, and I therefore sent it home by this Mail. It should cost little or nothing to put it in again. When sending it out, it would be well to drop a note to someone in the Foreign Office to know if they would send it out by their bag: they might otherwise throw it aside, as they appear to have done my papers. I shall see it put in myself *here*: but of course cannot tell whether they are willing at Whitehall to encumber the Mail bags with Student Interpreters' property.

I have been laid up the last three days by—mosquito bites! The cool weather suddenly disappeared; and in one night the mosquitos appeared in swarms. I had not put up mosquito curtains, and was totally unprepared for a midnight attack. I was bitten and sucked dry from head to foot. Face, hands and legs are in a terrible state. The bites all rise in large lumps, with an almost intolerable irritation. I was in bed the whole of the day before yesterday, as my clothes irritated me so much that I could not keep them on. Talk of fleas, or even bugs! they are to the mosquitos what the viper is to the boa-constrictor. There is another interesting blood-sucker here too—the sand fly which also feeds on human bodies. Its bite is not so bad as that of the mosquito in quality, but they are so insatiable that they bite over your whole person. I was really quite ill with the irritation and pain, but am recovering. Except the above arrivals, and that of a new Secretary Mr Farquhar, there is nothing new since I wrote the other day.

Believe me ever, your loving Son

To his Mother
Pi-Yün-ssŭ [1]—June 24th 1866

I received in due time your letters bearing date of the 18th of April, and the enclosures; for which many thanks. I am glad that Johnny has got lodgings that are likely to suit him. He's a gay young bachelor, with rooms of his own! The likeness you sent me of him is very good, though still not perfection but I am very glad to get it. I had only a "penny head" of him before.

You will see by the heading of this letter that I am at some place you don't know. I am at last installed in the much talked of temple, and it is its name that figures at the head of the sheet. I have spelt it as well as I can to give you an idea of the sound. The first two syllables are easy enough but I doubt if you can pronounce the third. It is a kind of hiss through the teeth, as if you were going to say the word *sith* (or *sidh*) and stopped just before the *th*. Try it all of you, and see what you can make of it. The temple is situated about half-way up a very high hill to the west of the city, and about seventeen miles from it. Below us there is a little village where we can get our eatables to buy. A beautiful stream runs through the grounds; and at one part of its coures is received into a stone-built basin where we bathe every day. There are I suppose more than one hundred different buildings in the place, which indeed occupies a very large area. My room is the highest up on the hill, and from its position is the coolest of the lot. I got it as having the last choice; for the other men took rooms in better repair; but a couple of dollars put it all to rights and I am quite comfortable. it is entirely open woodwork from ceiling to floor. I have it papered to the height of about six feet from the floor—and from that to the roof is covered with gauze to keep out mosquitos, and other bloodsuckers, and allow a free current through the room. The view from the top of the temple, is very extensive and very beautiful. There is one un-bounded plain as far as the eye can see, except when on a very bright day a few shadowy outlines of hills are seen on the far side of the city. The country is very beautiful now—the late rains have brought on the crops very fast, and the plain is almost all one map of green—*almost*, for in some places the wheat is quite golden, and in some it is already cut. The second crop in the early districts is generally rice. We are getting delicious vegetables and fruit now. We have peas, kidney beans,

1 In the Western Hills, the summer retreat for Westerners in Peking.

yams, lettuce, radish and potatoes: also apricots and cherries extremely cheap. But do what we can, we can't get any milk. There is no pasture here at all and cattle feeding is by [no] means a profitable speculation. I observed a flock of goats the other day and despatched my boy to inquire if they yielded milk and come to terms with the owner, but nothing has come of it yet.

From all this you will see that I am not likely to die immediately unless some unforeseen accident may put me on by back. I am working away at the language and have my teacher out here with me. We study most of the day in the open air under a summer house. The heat is very severe; and we cannot venture out except in the early morning or after six o'clock in the evenings for fear of sunstroke. Another month will see the excessive heat abated, and in the meantime we are in the most agreeable place to bear it. How I wish I could give you any idea of the place that would even make you imagine what it is like! I doubt if this could be done by anyone; but my attempts at description are indeed miserable. I am however keeping a sort of weekly journal, which I shall send you at the end of the autumn. When the heat moderates a little, two or three of us are going on a week's tour to the Great Wall, and one or two places of interest on the borders of Mongolia. I may also get up into the latter place in the autumn. I shall keep journals of my visits, and let you have them in a compact form, instead of piecemeal in letters.

You have of course long ago found out who my friends in Hong Kong were, as well as many other things about which you make inquiries. The news about Willie is indeed not very cheery: but I am sure something will turn up for him in the way of a rise, or a change for the better into some other line of business. For him to talk of coming to Peking if he *was* in China, is absolutely out of the question; for travelling in China is terribly expensive; and as he could have no reason for coming north but for the purpose of seeing me, it would be a very dear trip for him. But if he is anywhere near me when I go down to some of the ports, we will manage to meet, you may depend. And now to conclude and finish, let me tell you that I am well in health. As far as I have yet seen the climate of this place suits me well: I wish the whole of China were as healthy. A photographer is expected to visit Peking this summer; and if he comes I shall send you a picture of our mess, as we are going to get all done together. It has been the custom since the first students came; and two of our present number will be soon going from the Legation.

With love to all, not forgetting poor solitary *old James*, to whom I shall write often—believe me, darling Mother,

Your loving son.

To his Father,
Pi-Yün-ssŭ—June 25th, 1866

I received your very kind letter by last Mail, which contained the summary of my outfitting expenses; and I am indeed very grateful for your generous deduction of almost the half of the total. I had expected to have remitted to you before this time some money: but the difficulties of getting any channel of remittance are great as there is not a mercantile house nearer than Tientsing where a thing of the kind can be done. Before long however I shall find means of sending you the entire sum. Living here is not what one can call expensive, but on the other hand neither is it cheap, and as a newcomer I incurred at my outset more expenses than I expected and certainly more than I shall require to lay out next year. Thus by the time that I have sent you home £50, I shall not have saved anything this first year. I shall probably about Christmas, ask you to procure some things for me which I shall want next summer. My summer supply of clothing is not altogether sufficient; for I want such things as alpacca coats, more white clothes, and some other things, about which more again. I have already told you about the system of sending parcels as "Admiralty Packages" to us. How they are obtained I do not know; but all the outfitters in London can get an order to send parcels that have been bought from them. Parcels for me should be addressed to the care of the Consul at Shanghai, who will forward them to the Legation. Perhaps it might be well to get Johnnie who is in London to procure my things that I may want from some of the regular outfitters, who would then send them and save you all trouble. But I shall communicate again with you on this subject.

Meanwhile be assured that I shall by the first opportunity (and I am inquiring for one every day) send you home as much money as I can amass till the £50 is paid off.

My mother will let you know how I am getting on at the temple. I find it a delightful life, and shall be sorry to return again to the city.

My mother hopes that by this time I can talk *"pigeon"*. Tell her that I am surprised and grieved to hear that she imagines me capable of such an atrocity! No. I can now talk a little Chinese, and am in a fair way of being able one day to talk a great deal. No Chinaman here can speak a syllable of English; consequently no "pigeon" is spoken. It is only at the ports where few of the English speak Chinese, that the natives pick up any English. I have some good opportunities of conversing and hearing conversation with the Buddhist priests of the temple.

They are a well educated but not a high class of men. I believe our teachers are of better family and position in general; still they can talk Chinese and talk it well: and therefore I occasionally try a little conversation with them. I find it much more difficult to understand what they say than to talk myself. The only remedy for this is constant conversation with the teacher upon all subjects.

Please let me know any of Willy's movements that he may tell you about. I am very anxious to know what he does, and whether he is getting promotion, and in fact all about him.

Give my love to all at home and all "inquiring-for-me" friends. I am collecting my ideas for an epistle to Drummond, who I hope is working hard at school. Believe me, ever and always your loving son

To his Mother

Pi-Yün-ssŭ—July 8th 1866

Your letter and that of my father arrived safely last week. They bore the date of the 1st or 2nd of May. I am glad that my Shanghai despatch seems to have given you an idea of how I was getting on, although any recollection of it is that it was a poor enough production. But I know that you would not like to read any more than I should like to write letters written for effect; and if I tell you as well as I can what I am doing you are sufficiently pleased with the attempt. Your news was all pleasant, and I am glad that you are all so well; and above all that my dear father has no more annoyance from his enemy, the *lumbago*. I hope you have gone to the shore some place, if it should be only for a month. It always did you good; and you must feel very lonely in town when most of your friends, and Bella and the children are at the sea-side. By the way you do not mention having had any further renewal of the offer for the old house in College Square.

The arrival of the Cape party will be something for you to think about, especially if any of them put up with you. Besides they will bring you the latest news of Willy. He does not seem to be in high spirits about himself, poor fellow, from what you tell me; but I trust he will get some better situation before long.

Tell my father, that I have not time to answer his letter by this Mail: but I shall do so by the next; and by the same shall write to Mr Coates, and to the Allens, if possible. I should already have given you a much fuller account of the Legation and its inmates but one cannot form an opinion of it at once. I shall however comply with my father's request, by next Mail.

I am sorry Johnny feels so lonely as he does, but I think he will soon grow accustomed to the place, and in time like it. I never heard of anyone yet, who after a fair trial disliked living in London. He will miss his fortnight at the shore for the first time. I feel the want of my *bathe* awfully: though there is a capital bath, a stream of clear water in a marble paved basin, always fresh and cool; but nothing can make up for the want of the accustomed swim. That will be one advantage the ports have, if they have a good many drawbacks.

My newspapers, and *Christian Unitarians* all came by last Mail, and McKean and I have been reading them for the last few days. There is really an immense amount of news in one of these papers; and as it is all *news* to us, we devour it eagerly. Sir Rutherford has had an influx of visitors this last month. The Judge of the Supreme Court at Shanghai, Sir Edmund Hornby, and several officers and gentlemen came to Tientsing in HMS *Barossa* and thence to Peking where they were entertained by the minister. We had visits from several of the distinguished guests, and did our best to entertain them hospitably.

And my dear Mother, forgive the shortness and want of news in this letter. I have nothing new to tell you.

By the by, you say "I enclose a letter from Meg." You did not do so, however. I must exhort you, painful as it is, *Never to promise more than you can perform*! It is a good rule.

Love to my Father, to Andrew, Bella and Sandy, and to all friends in the country: and believe me ever

Your loving son

To his Mother

Pi-Yün-ssŭ—July 22nd 1866

You will learn from my note to my father that no Foreign Office bag arrived by this last Mail, and I cannot therefore answer anything in the letters—which I am sure you wrote. I was anxious to learn anything about Willy and his movements, as well as to hear the ordinary home news. I have nothing of interest to tell you by this Mail and my letter will be necessarily short. Still at the temple, and enjoying its cool shade and retirement. I find I can do twice as much work here as in the Legation—where at this season the heat is intolerable. My teacher was ill last week and was obliged to enter the walls, as they call going into the city: so I had not so much work as I ought; but I am making progress and a few days' slack work will not matter much. The last Mail brought out orders for a good many changes in the service; and a good many men get promotion. Among others, our oldest student here, Mowat, has been ordered to Han Kow, on the Yangtsi, where his salary is to be £375. That will probably be my step also: not a very brilliant one: but a step, ma'am! a step to something better. We are going to give the man a little dinner before he goes, and I go into the city tomorrow for that purpose. He has not been popular; but we are unwilling to let him think that it has been through any fault of ours. The visitors to the Legation are all gone again, and we shall [not] see any more, probably, for another year. Lowder, Sir Rutherford's step-son was examined almost a year ago, to get into the consular service as a student. His papers went home: and he has received answer that he cannot be admitted. Sir Edmund Hornby, of the Supreme Court in Shanghai, has however given him the situation of Interpreter to that Court, at a salary of £400, rising by degrees to £1200. He could have had any interpreter in the service for that situation; but he preferred Lowden, who has been working at Chinese since the 1st of October last, and at the present time I have overtaken him myself. What it is to be a *Minister's* son!—(I don't mean a *Presbyterian* minister. If that was of any use, I should have the same chance.)

I told you that my windows were made of gauze, and as I am writing there are China-men staring and gaping in at me. When I have finished this I shall go out and try conclusions with them; that is to say bow them out. My budget of newspapers has kept me in constant reading since I got them. I do now what I never did before—read the leading articles in the *Whig*! Tell me who is the new editor. I saw by the paper the birth of a daughter (or was it a *son*?) to Francis Dalzell Finlay Esq, which you did not mention. Please tell all the members of my family, that letters from them will be acceptable.

I hope James is now not so lonely as he was. Give him my love and tell him to keep up his heart! Love to Bella and Terraceans; to Andrew and John, and the the rest of your numerous family: and to yourself, my dearest mother.

And now for the Chinamen!

Your loving son

P.S.—I inclose you a memorandum about the Admiralty packages. I shall want one out by next January, but of that more before then. I forgot to say that Mowat gets me the order on his way through Shanghai and will post it from that place—F.K.P.

To his Mother

Pi-Yün-ssŭ—August 4th 1866

I have to answer by this Mail the last *two* of your home budgets, which arrived within a few days of each other. You seemed to be all getting on famously when you wrote. There was noting particular in your first letter which was not in answer to one of mine, except the enclosures from Andrew Johnny and Maggie. I am glad that Andrew is going in for horse exercise. I hope to hear soon of his doing some tremendous feat in the hunting-fields if he takes to that kind of riding.

Johnnie seems to like his new place. I had a letter from him by the same Mail; and from it and yours I see that if he has once extricated himself from the toils of the Prestons, he will be quite at home. The last Mail bore date of the last of May and was in answer to my first letter for Peking. I am very much obliged to you all for not only looking on my wretched letters with lenient eye, but for stretching a point to say you are pleased with them. Such as they are, you shall have one by every Mail. My photographs—four of my own ugly mug, and two of my father came safely to hand. I quite agree with you that Magill's *carte* of my father is the best ever taken of him. I am very glad to have him in different attitudes. I have now Ward's, Gibson's and Magill's.

I see you have had the sense to go to the sea-side for some little time, after all. I hope that my father and James may get Uncle Classon's house for a month or six weeks. It will do them both ever so much good.

From the *Illustrated London News* report

The Chinese Mission, at present in London, consists of the Commissioner Pin-Ta-Chun (Ta-Chun being simply the Chinese for His Excellency), his son, Quang-Ying, and three secretaries, with Mr Edward Bowra, Secretary and Interpreter; Mr. Des Champs [*sic*] who fills a similar position in France; and Major J. Brine, R.E., attached by the Foreign Office in London, as Aide-de-camp. The Commissioner, who has held many and important positions in the Empire, is sixty-four years of age, and by birth a Tartar. He is a man of wide and enlightened views, and at present holds the position of Secretary to the Board of Foreign Affairs at Pekin. He has considerable literary powers, and since he has been in London has been busily employed in writing poetry—prose being, as he remarks, entirely inadequate to express his feelings, not only at the European wonders of art and science, but at the uniformly courteous and kind reception he has met with in this country. On his return his office will be to draw up a report of what he has seen, and to give his advice as to the introduction of European arts and civilisation into China, or any modifications of customs which his intercourse with the outer barbarians may have suggested. He has visited Windsor, and was present at the Royal ball at Buckingham Place. He is staying at the New United Hotel, Charles-street, Haymarket. After leaving England he will visit St. Petersburg, Copenhagen, Stockholm, Berlin, Brussels, Hamburg, Lübeck, and Paris; indeed, he is accredited to all the Powers which have treaties with China, including America, which he will visit on his way home, crossing to China via San Francisco and the Pacific, touching at Japan and the Society Islands; thus having performed a voyage round the world, which it is probable no Chinese—certainly no other Chinese official—has done since the commencement of the Chinese era. We have reason to congratulate not only China but Europe upon this mission. Its significance is really vast, and may be best understood if we regard it as a pledge that the old policy of isolation is broken through; that the incrustation of Chinese pride, coupled with ignorance and abhorrence of the Western peoples, will gradually fall off; and that, finally, the Chinese empire, strong by the honesty and ingenuity of its people, their patience, industry, and abundant resources, will be brought, in our own days, to sit at the councils and take its share in the progress of the brotherhood of nations. This result is owing partly to the generous forbearance of foreign Powers, who hesitated to take advantage of the weakness to which China was reduced, and to the individual exertions of Messrs. Wade and Hart, who for many years have been endeavouring to bring about this result. Mr. Wade is Secretary of Legation in China; and Mr. Hart is Inspector-General of the Imperial Customs at Pekin, and virtually Foreign Minister.

Our Portrait is from a photograph by Mr. Disderi.

6 'The Chinese Commissioner Pin-Ta-Chun':
Illustrated London News, 23 June 1866

A telegram across Russia brought us news of the European outbreak,[1] and the opening victories of the Austrians over the Prussians,
somewhere in Bohemia, and over the Italians at Verona. It is to be
hoped that our country will not be dragged into the hostilities. These
accounts that I have heard may be untrue. I am waiting for my papers
but I hear the result of the actions. Only one *Whig* came by this Mail.
It bore date of the 2nd of June, but contained no news of the war.—No
Christian Unitarians. They will all come in good time.

There is great indignation in the Legation that *Pin*,[2] one of the
Chinamen who accompanied Hart to England, has had an audience of
the Queen. Pin is a very low mandarin, who does not come to call on
Mr Wade without first asking Murray or Brown if he will be received.
He got his rank conferred on him when he left China in order that he
might keep up a respectable appearance. The fact of the Queen giving
audience to the Chinese first, will not help her minister to an audience
of the emperor when he comes of age. As I told you before, Alcock is
not a man of much gumption, and he may not insist sufficiently on the
importance of such a step; now the French will certainly do so, and
enforce the demand by an army, so that in all probability we, who were
the first power to make a treaty with the Chinese, will step in through
the breach the French have made. Thirteen French Roman Catholic
Missionaries have been savagely murdered in Corea, and the French
have declared war against the country, and send up gunboats and
troops. They will teach the Coreans a lesson not soon to be forgotten.
Their minister here is a regular little firebrand who stops at nothing.

I wish there was anything to tell you that would interest you; but
life here is monotonous; and will be so till the days grow cool. At
present we have great heat and thunder in the evening, but no rain. You
have had an unusually long drought for the north of Ireland. I scarcely
recollect dry weather at home lasting for a month unbroken.

Bella has of course found out from books before this, that she was
right about the jack-daw. I scarcely even saw a jack-daw that was not
grey headed. If she had noticed the eye of the bird, it would have settled
the point at once: a jack-daw's eye is a beautiful pearl eye; not black
as the rest of the corbie genus. We have crows here, white on the back
of the neck and breast.[3] There are also ravens,[4] but not many of them.

1 The Austro-Prussian War.
2 Pin-ch'un, a minor Manchu official employed as secretary in the Chinese depart-
    ment of customs; he led a group which Hart took with him to Europe in 1866.
3 Collared crow.
4 Jungle crow.

There is a great want of song birds. I have only, I think, heard two kinds singing wild. One was a red and blue bird,[1] the size of a blackbird that whistled in the same way. The other is a little grey fellow,[2] like a hedge-sparrow but lighter in the colour that indeed can scarcely be said to sing, but to twitter and chirp. The soldiers of the imperial army go about everywhere, with tame birds on their finger, or tied to a stick which the man carries while the bird sits perched on it. There is a pretty large parade ground for the solders, near us, and I have seen them practising. The great thing seems to become expert with the bow and arrow. They have a long straight trench dug, and near the middle but about fifty yards, away from it a target is put up. The soldier rides down the trench at full speed; and when opposite the target lets fly the arrow. It looks well; but is not of much use in modern warfare. The cavalry have ponies; very small ones: and they are indeed a contemptible set of men—badly dressed: and I believe worse paid.

August 9—I stopped here the other day, waiting until another day should have passed; thinking I might have something to add; but nothing has occurred, worthy of repetition. I shall write to my father to thank him for the photographs and the Hebrew books which he has promised to send me. The money order with I have commissioned Mr Mowat to procure for me may possibly only go home by this Mail. This is the more likely as I have not yet got the duplicate (or triplicate) of it from the Bank. I hope soon to send you home some more.

The heat is still very intense, and the last three nights we have had terrific thunder and lightning. The fall of rain that accompanies these storms cools the air in the morning, but at midday the sun is as warm as ever. There are only three of us now at the temple. McKean prefers the Legation and has left us. Harvey and McClatchie are my companions here. McClatchie is a nephew of Sir Harry Parkes, the minister in Japan. His father is a consular chaplain at some of the ports. I should like to stay at Peking for a year or two over the regular time; but not much longer. There are only two posts about the Legation that could be filled by a *sucking consul*—accountant, and assistant Chinese secretary; the former I should not like to hold, for there is no chance of promotion; the language is not required to do the duties; and a man who has a good knowledge of the language has far more chance of getting on by working in the consulates. The second post is so well

1 Blue rock thrush.
2 Tree sparrow.

filled by Brown that no one need for a long time think of getting into it.

Love to the boys: and the Murray Terrace household; to the country people and all friends; from your ever loving son

To his Father

Pi-Yün-ssŭ—August 9th 1866

Your long letter of the 31st of May reached me by last Mail, having come taking something less than two months. The photographs inclosed, arrived safely also. Many thanks for sending them so promptly. I am greatly delighted with Magill's likeness of you. It is by far the best and most pleasing likeness of you that I have yet seen. The papers and magazines arrive generally at intervals of two months, and each arrival brings enough to keep me in reading till the next. All the important news I see in the Legation reading room, where we take all the first rate periodicals and papers; but I am always interested in everything that concerns the old place and I prize the *Whig* quite as highly as the *Times*.

You mentioned some time ago having had an offer for the house in College Square but since then I have had no account of any arrangement made. Please let me know if you come to any.

I shall be very glad to get the Hebrew books and whatever hints you can write for me and when I go back to the city I shall begin the study, if the books have arrived. An hour, or an hour and half a day will take nothing off my time for Chinese studies, and will be of considerable use in helping me to a slight knowledge of Hebrew. We have an excellent little library here, containing little or no trash, and a great many most select works, and I am never without something good to read. I am by this time able to talk a good deal of ordinary talk; and I neglect no opportunity of giving my knowledge an airing. Talking with the teacher is not a good way, at least not a quick way of learning new words and phrases; for the most of [them] having been about the legation for a long time, have begun to adapt their conversation to the attainments of the pupil. They know in a short time his stock of phrases, and keep within them when they talk to him. This is however still practising what one knows and that is of importance. As soon as I go back to the city I shall get you some really nice Chinese books, if any such are to be had in Peking. I have seen several; but I am not sure if they can be readily bought here. I shall find out through my teacher, and get him to bring me some or tell me where I can see them. I shall also send you a Chinese manuscript book which in my opinion is far nicer. The types here are not moveable, but cut on a solid plate, which makes books rarer than they otherwise would be. Labour however is cheap; and I do not think the books are dear.

In this letter I send you a sheet containing an exercise drawn up by Mr Wade, with the help of teachers, for the students. I shall translate some of the sentences in idiomatic English and then take the Chinese words in order and give the English for each. It is merely to let you see what we do. The most of the Chinese books, indeed all, have the pages stitched with the open part at the back, and the closed edge at the front.

Please excuse the want of news in this letter, and again accept my best thanks for the photographs: and believe me, my dear Father,

Your loving son

To his Mother

Pi-Yün-ssŭ—Sunday August 19th 1866

Though the Mail does not go out for at least another week, I commence my letter now, as it will probably be the last one I shall write from this delightful temple. The weather has set in quite cool and delicious; and though we could now enjoy ourselves much more than when the heat lasted, living in the Legation is endurable: and we had agreed that when we could say *that* we should pack up our trunks and be off.† Through the remainder of the autumn we can occasionally take a run out for a few days at a time. I have been working hard out here; but I intend to set to work with still more ferocity when I am again settled in my own old quarters. The quiet of this place is greatly in its favour; but there are interruptions constantly occurring, with Chinese visitors, European visitors coming to see the place and the delay of the teachers who go in every Sunday to the city, and do not come out sometimes till Tuesday. You can see how far I wrote down the first page on August 19. [See †.]

Some interruption occurred to stop me: the Mail arrived yesterday, bringing letters dated 17th June from you and Johnnie and Miss Knowles. Many thanks for the inclosures. The *cards* are the very pink of perfection! Your news is all pleasant except the Institution affair.[1] The trip to London will have done my father much good, I am sure: and James is certain to enjoy himself. How Maggy delighted in the Crystal Palace expedition, with such a guide, I can well imagine. From what Johnnie tells me, and an expression in Andrew's note, I fear you have not been so well as usual. I hope you will take great care of yourself: a month at Larne would do you all the good in the world. If you had a month of Peking weather instead of dreary rainy weather —as Miss Knowles describes it to me—you would [have] some heat in your bones.

During the last three weeks we have had a good many Europeans from the south up here. In the month of August, the hottest in the year at the southern parts, those who wish to escape fever and sunstroke take a trip north, and generally end the tour by an excursion into Mongolia. The Legation and the Alcock's temple are at the disposal of all such visitors. We are to have the prince [Duc?] d'Alençon, over here soon from Japan. He has been travelling about there for sometime with another follower of distinction whose name I forget. By the way I heard Wade (in speaking of a man here you never *Mr* him) speaking of Rennie's book.[2] He said he disliked excessively having his name dragged into every page; and the amount of private conversation that occurred at Sir Frederick's table transferred into the book was a sufficient proof of the ignorance of the man. I have merely looked at the book, and can not therefore say anything about it but it seems to be as interesting as any book on the subject *can* be. They must all be dry if they detail the truth. Our friend Sir John Bowring (Knight)[3] did not write to Sir Rutherford Alcock and, I am rather glad he did not, as no introduction of the sort was necessary and coming from him would be in all other respects than as an introduction quite useless. He is not thought any thing of in China; indeed *quite* the reverse, as the lady replied when asked if her husband was an attorney. Mr Mercer, the acting Governor of Hong Kong said to me very quietly when I mentioned that Sir John had told me so and so, "Oh yes; but he tells a great deal more than he knows." He distinctly told me he had been in Peking and that the cold had driven him out of it. Now he never was

1 A dispute between two masters, John Carlisle and Revd Isaiah Steen.
2 Sir Richard Temple Rennie, 1839–1903, barrister, practised in supreme court, Shanghai, judge in Japan 1878, chief justice of supreme court in China, Japan and Shanghai 1882.
3 Sir John Bowring, 1792–1874, had a varied career as writer, traveller and MP; served in China as plenipotentiary; governor of Hong Kong 1854.

in the capital in all his life, as every one here knows. The hoary old sinner!

The boots that were sent by the first steamer have not yet arrived. They would, however, go round the Cape, and would be much longer on the road. I hope they may all arrive before the winter sets in.

I think I have already told you that McKean improves much on acquaintance, though he never lays aside a certain reserve of manner. He is not only quite disposed to be friendly but anxious to oblige in every way. His rooms and mine are in the same house; and we are thus brought into contact in many matters. For work we both keep pretty close together; the result probably of over close intercourse: for the one knows thus how far the other has gone, and takes care not to let him away with a start. My father or one of the boys might write to Mr Storey[1] for my degree, with the University seal. He was to have sent it to me after the examination came off but neglected it. You need scarcely send it out to me, as I do not want it here. Keep it till I come to claim it. If William Rothwell[2] does not go into College this year, you might find some of my examination papers lying about, and let him have them. He may get from them an idea of the sort of thing he may expect. May he do more in the scholarship line than I did: however scholarships are not the only inducements to go to College. My life here is just a continuation of my College career: but with the exception of lectures and examinations. You all seem to think it strange that I am thinking of taking up Hebrew again. If it were to study it with a view to master the language you might be rather astonished; but I only mean to take an hour or two at it now and again; that when I have no longer any time at my disposal for any study, but the work of my regular routine I may have made some advancement in a language that I have already dabbled in. And in the mean time I expect to find it if not an amusement, at least a light second course, after the heavy Chinese that forms the bulk of my (intellectual) repast.

No more news. My papers and *Christian Unitarians* did not arrive; and out here I hear no further news of the European outbreak. I got a duplicate of the bill which I sent home and find it was only £14.14. The value of the dollar had fallen in Shanghai. I shall by Christmas have paid up the rest to you.

Enclosed is a list of things to be got for me, and sent out as an Admiralty package, of which you have the regulations. If sent by the

---

1 George Johnstone Storey, FRS, professor of natural philosophy, Queen's College, Galway; secretary Queen's College, Belfast.
2 Lived at 5 Murray's Terrace.

second Mail in January it would reach me without being detained by the ice. Get the bill made out in my name and I will forward the payment, either direct or through you—but don't you pay for them. All respectable tradesmen will give credit for at least six or nine months.

You may think I am wanting too much: but there is nothing in the list that I can well do without and I shall get no more clothes while I am in Peking. If James gets measured for me, they ought to fit well. Love to my father—to all the boys and Maggie from

Your ever loving son

To his Mother

British Legation, Peking—September 8th 1866

I told you in my last letter that I expected soon to leave the temple; and I have not broken my word as the heading of this sheet tells. The weather has set in cool and fresh as it was before the two months of excessive heat, and more resembles spring than autumn. We should have been obliged to come in however—*nolens volens* (or *-entes* as I am writing to a Latin scholar) for two men of our number have been ordered off to the ports. The consulates are very short of men just now, and these men were sent off before they had been here their legitimate time. One has been only out ten months. Of course you can understand that when a man is to make his position, by his knowledge of the language it is very hard to deprive him of the only means in his reach for studying it; for in the South Pekingese teachers are not to be had; and to take one down or take a local one is far out of the reach of men who have only advanced their first step. So much for local matters.

Your letter and that of my father with Maggie's inclosed, arrived all right the other day. They were of the date of July 2nd, I can readily understand why you have not got my second and third letters from this place. True enough the Mail goes every fortnight; but if the courier misses the steamer at Tientsing or the latter arrives too late for the P and O at Shanghai, the thing is explained. Add to this that letters may lie kicking up and down the Foreign Office for a week or so; you must however have since been satisfied that I have written to you by every Mail that has gone out, and I mean to do so. If my letters give you anything like the pleasure that yours give me I would not willingly deprive you of them.

My first act on coming into the city was to ask Murray about a book such as my father wants; and the latter—(no the *former*—just like me)—picked me up two capital ones at an auction of books belonging to a man in the Russian Legation. One is a small edition of one portion of the works of Confucius in good print, and of immense antiquity; the other is a collection of Chinese plays with wood-cuts. The former is in the square type: the latter in the "manuscript" type, if I may so speak, it is although printed, a fac-simile of the ordinary manuscript of the Chinese. They were got ridiculously cheap. I shall take the first opportunity of sending them home, with a few other *curios*. If I can manage to translate myself, or get them translated, a scene or two from the plays, you may be amused at it. I shall also find out the date of the printing and all ascertainable particularly about both of them.

I am getting on with the language and am about to begin a novel which has been translated by Sir John Davis,[1] called *The Fortunate Union*. There are translations of it in the library, and I can get along by myself for a little every day, and then go over the day's work with the teacher. Wade has prepared more exercises of a more difficult sort in the form of dialogues which also I shall be at. I have done his first set and gone over them till I absolutely know them by heart. They contain (the first set) a thousand characters and upwards—and with the addition of 214 radicals which are not included in the exercises, I ought to know at least 1200 characters; not to mention "a good few" that I have picked up out of other books. If your letter did not contain very much news, mine must be a very brilliant production; but the study of Chinese is calculated, I find, to batter all ideas out your head except that of self: so don't be surprised if you find that in a short time I forget *you*!

There have been a good many changes in the service as I told you, and in a little time there will be more. A good many of the old Consuls are going off the hooks in another year or thereabouts and a chance is thus given to those who have been some time in the service. Of myself I can give you no news. I am growing a beard which is expected to eclipse anything of the kind that has yet appeared in Peking. The visiting cards came by the last Mail all safe. I have not yet got either the first or the second package of boots; but expect them in due time. As regards the list of things I sent home for, I don't think that I am

1 Sir John Francis Davis, 1795–1890, governor of Hong Kong 1844–48; wrote several works on China and translated Chinese novels.

going in for horsey-ness. But one cannot do without riding sometimes; and it is cheaper to have the proper appurtenances than to wear out good clothes. We can hire good ponies here for 1/6 a day! and I ride a good deal at that rate. The other items are necessaries, not luxuries.

I cannot write to my father as the Mail is leaving three days earlier than the fixed time; and I have been taken short for time even to write this. I shall answer Maggie's letter duly. I was very very sorry indeed to hear of Dr Craik's[1] death. He was one of the nicest men I ever was under, and I had the highest respect—I may say veneration—for him. I hope there was a sufficient number of students in town, to make a respectable appearance at his funeral. If I recollect right the last time I saw him was at Mr Allen's dinner party: if not the last, certainly almost the last, time I spoke to him. I have not got my papers by this Mail and have seen no details of his life; merely a brief obituary notice in the *Illustrated News*.

I am glad James is gone over to London to enjoy himself, as he is sure to do. By this time Johnny will know all the reports of the men of music and of the other fine arts, and can take James about to them all. I am surprised at Willy's silence, but he may be on his way home. Perhaps he may be among you when you get this.

I shall make you up a box after the winter containing some Chinese curios, in China and other ware; and a few furs which are to be had here [are] very good—I am going to send the boys a stuff for winter waistcoats greatly in use here: the dressed fleece of a newly born lamb: it is of a grey colour, all close with little curls, and as soft as down—and I shall look out for other things as well.

This brings me to the end of my letter. I apologise for the short and confused way in which I have written this but time and tide wait for no man. Give warm love to all at home from

Your ever loving son

To his Mother

British Legation, Peking—September 28th 1866

I cannot do more than write you a short scrawl by this Mail and that for two reasons. The Legation has been filled with naval officers of

---

1 George Lillie Craik, 1798–1866; LL.D. University of St Andrews; professor of History and English Literature, Queen's College, Belfast, 1849–66.

HMS *Princess Charlotte*; who have been thrown upon our tender mercies, to shew them about the city for the last week; and the Mail starts a day before its time, and has taken me by surprise. I can however tell you that I am getting on well; and am well in health though much tired in body with the last few days knocking about. Your last letters arrived all right; and a few cards contained in them also. I have not yet got either of my parcels of boots; but I expect them every day: meanwhile I am getting [on] tolerably well with what I have. By this time I suppose you have all got back from Larne, and settled down in the usual old way.

I hope the stay has done you all good. Was it in our own old house or in Mr Kirkpatrick's that you were? The weather makes all the difference between a pleasant and an unpleasant stay at a place; and if you have had good weather, I am sure you have got on well. We have had fine weather the last three weeks. Cold in the mornings and evenings, and very warm in the day-time: but the dust in the streets is abominable.—Only that the mad-cap navy men were here, I should scarcely ever stir out of the Legation. In another month however, there will be a variety—*much*!

Sir Rutherford is at present entertaining HRH le Duc d'Alençon; a grandson of Louis Philippe, it is said; so that explains why he does not go to the French minister. I have only seen him for a minute and cannot tell much from that. His Secretary, Baron (?) Bach is also here, and a swarm of officers and Mids. The more distinguished guests are out at the temple, and the others are billeted about the Legation and the city. Some of them mess with the Secretaries and some with us. In return for all these civilities, the smoking men in the Legation will get presents of navy tobacco: and there are even dark whispers that if navy rum were appreciated, it could be sent to us. They are all good fellows, and inclined to see the best side of everything.—You can't please them better than arm them with whips, and let them loose on a colony of street dogs. In a few seconds the howls (of the latter) rend the sky, and not a dog can be had for half a mile round. This is an innocent, and also a useful amusement; for these hounds when once flogged generally remember the appearance of a foreign devil, and avoid them.

Tell Drummond I am glad he has got a dog; but he might have succeeded in procuring a more useful animal than a Japanese—what? terrier?—lap dog? most probably all these useful breeds combined.— Tell him to take it out for exercise: if not for its own sake, for that of the "lovely girls" who gave it him. Heigh O! there are no such things here!

Give my love to my father, and all the others on both sides of the Square. Tell Mary and Jane that I am on the look out for husbands for them; and shall expect them as soon as I can find two big enough—I am dearest Mother,

Ever Your loving son

To his Father

British Legation, Peking—October 29th 1866

Forgive if you can my apparent neglect of you and my dear Mother by the last Mail and the short and hurried letter that you have by this. I have been in Mongolia, on a tour with Sir Eric Farquhar, one of our Secretaries of Legation and McKean. We were away three weeks, and during that time a Mail went out. I had written you a letter previously to be posted by one of our men, who unfortunately forgot to do so, and I am afraid you might think that something was wrong. By next Mail I shall send you a detailed account of my trip. I kept a diary, and can enlarge it so as to present a respectable appearance. Some of our exploits may afford you a laugh; and if they do, I think *that* quite worth any trouble (and very little trouble it has been) that I have taken to write them down. The Mail is going out in a few minutes; and my pen-hand has been somewhat cramped by guiding a Tartar pony for three weeks and refuses to scratch any more. I have received your last Mail all right, and a letter from Willy, in which the poor fellow speaks in the same breath of coming out to China, and of going home to see you! but winds up by assuring me that he will not come here, till he has first seen you all at home. I am going to write him a long letter this week; but it may be that he has ere this gone back to dear old Belfast, and gladdened you all by his unexpected arrival.

My *odd* boots have come by this last Mail, and fit in every way well. Captain Nolan has my sincere *blessings*, for forgetting my parcel: but it will all come right in the end.

Three more students have arrived by this last Mail; but I have not yet had time to study them. You shall have the result of my cogitations by the next Mail. And now with fondest love to my mother, and all the boys, and Maggie, believe me,

Your ever loving son

To his Mother
Saturday night—November 10th (11 o'clock)

Dearest Mother,

I am just told this minute that the Mail, which was announced to go on Monday morning will be made up tonight in a few minutes. I had not yet finished my account of my tour, but hope to sent it by next Mail. I am very much vexed about this unexpected occurrence but cannot help it. Your letters of September 4th came all right and many thanks for them. I shall write to all the boys by next Mail. I am well myself, and hard at work.—My newspapers and *Christian Unitarians* came all right. When one has only two minutes to write, not much news can be told, and I hear them calling to me to send in my letters; so good bye. Love to my father and all the boys, and Bella; and believe me, dear Mother though in haste,

Ever your loving son,

To his Mother
British Legation—November 27th 1866

I am again by my want of forethought cut down to a very short letter. I had almost finished my account of my Mongolian tour, but do not wish to send if off without another look over. I have got my par[-cel] containing books and boots and papers. Many thanks for them. Your letters were all pleasant. Thank the boys and Andrew and Maggie for remembering me. I cannot write to them by this—but shall by the next Mail. Language is progressing and that is the chief thing. Wade left us yesterday to return to England, and Hart has arrived from Shanghai with his wife: I am going to call on them this week. For myself I am well; never was better; I weight 10 st 1½ lb which is great novelty for me. When I left home I was 9 st 3 lbs. I am sorry this is so short a letter, but faithfully promise you a longer one next. Love to *all*: from fondly Yours.

To his Mother

British Legation—December 18th 1866

I duly received your letters by the October Mail, and should reply to them separately, but may not have time. The river has frozen up and this Mail goes down overland to Chin Kiang, whence it will be sent by steamer to Shanghai and thence home: and as there [is] about this time always a press of work in the Chancery with the despatches I have scarcely had a minute to myself. I have not done a word of Chinese the last week and have been copying, docketing and dictating till all is blue. I had intended to send you a long letter but I hope you will be content with this when you know that I cannot make a longer one.

I am glad you have received the money I sent. There was very little of it; but a better day is coming. I mentioned in my last letter that I had got the box all right. I think I have not had occasion to put on the boots yet.

Mr and Mrs Hart have arrived here. I have called and seen the lady who is a very nice person indeed. She comes from Portadown or somewhere near. She will be quite an acquisition to the Peking community.—Mr Wade has left us to go to Shanghai for the winter, and home in the Spring. I do not care for him personally but I am sorry he is gone for he coached us in the language. Brown holds his situation till a new man is appointed. Except this, and the information that I am well and strong, I have nothing more to say.

Christmas is soon coming on: and I suppose you are making preparation for a family gathering. We all dine with her ladyship on that day. From this time forth till the spring, the Mails go so irregularly that I shall wish you many happy returns of the season now; and not wait till it arrives (Christmas day I mean).

Remember me to all friends and relations. Tell the boys and Maggie that I shall write to them all soon. Give my love to my father, and tell him that he deserves better treatment than he has had from me of late—but that I really cannot help it.

By the way I am *twenty* now. I forgot the day till it was past and gone or I should have drunk my own health. If you did not drink mine, drink it when you get this. And now I must pull in. In future I shall commence my letters directly the Mail is gone; and then nothing can interfere with them. I have my notes of my tour north lying in my desk: but they are not yet fit for sending home. I shall also set to work on them this week.

· So now good bye, excuse this hurried letter if you can—I am really ashamed to send it home as a reply to yours, which are so long and so pleasant. But no matter. I have told you why. Believe me darling Mother,

Ever your loving

To his Mother

British Legation, Peking—January 4th 1866

I have not received any letters from you since I last wrote, owing to the frozen state of the river. I hope that mine have reached you more regularly. Christmas has come and gone; and New Year's Day too without anything remarkable: a sad contrast to the same season at home. Sir Rutherford entertained us all on Christmas day; and in the forenoon there were two jugglers brought to his house for the amusement of the Legationers. They performed exceedingly well; and helped us to pass what would have been otherwise a very dull day. The weather is now extremely cold, and all the water in and about Peking frozen hard. I have had some good skating, but the dust here gets on the ice and makes it rough. The Chinese skate well, those who do skate, but it is not a very prevalent amusement. Among the Bannermen of the Imperial army there are some thousands who are obliged to skate well; no doubt that if an emergency occurs, they may be able to carry despatches with speed.—I really have nothing *new* to tell you, but the same *old* rhyme (rather a bull that!) that I am well and working hard. The latter is rather a new sensation to me, you'll allow. I had intended to write you all letters at this time, when you will all be at home together; but I have nothing to fill up more than one with. So my darling mother, you must give them all my dear love, and ask them to forgive my neglect. I hope the boys had as fine a day for their Christmas as I had here. I know of old how we used to steal out of bed and look out of the window in the morning, to see what sort of day it was. We have had no rain here for, I think four months. The Chinese themselves say that this is an unusually mild season; but I should like to see a severe one if that be the case. Still I am well wrapped up both day and night and the cold can't kill me, as long as that goes on.

When you write in answer to this, tell me about everyone—both in your own circle and out of it; and how the congregation is getting on; not forgetting Mr Darbishire.

And so good bye, I have written myself out, and have fairly nothing more to say. Again, give my father, the boys and Maggie—the Taylors, Allens and all of them my dear love. And with as much to yourself as ever you like, believe me, dearest Mother,

Ever your own

To his Mother

British Legation—November 24th 1866 to January 12th 1867

After many disappointments, it will be a satisfaction to you to get from me a letter of respectable length. I told you in my last hasty scrawl that the departure of the Mail was hurried so as to leave me no time to write anything; but I duly received all your letters; and was not a little glad to get them. I also received the other day the Admiralty packages containing my boots and books. Many thanks for them all. I hope that I shall soon be able to send you a box of things, and I am collecting a number of little articles that may please you as giving an idea of Chinese ingenuity. I have not yet accomplished much in the saving of money for little expenses are every now and then cropping up, which I cannot avoid: but before long you shall have, I hope something respectable.

I had letters from the boys by the last Mail and from Maggie. I cannot write to them all by this Mail, but tell them I shall not forget them. It is very very good of them to write to me so often, and I shall do all I can to reply to them in time. I mentioned some letters ago that I was on a tour in Mongolia, that "undiscovered country"; but I have returned from its bourne safe and sound. It may help to make this letter interesting to give an account of the journey and how we performed it. I have a few notes, but found they were too scanty to make anything like a journal; and I think you will enjoy them as much in the form of a letter: so here goes.

We left the Legation on a Sunday morning very early, accompanied by a caravan of mules. There was a mule-chair for the bedding and the luggage was put on packs. Farquhar's boy, my boy and the former's Greek valet formed the menial part of the equipage, and McKean, Farquhar and myself were the distinguished party. We rode ponies and the boys mules. We made that day for Nankow, "the southern pass"—which is the nearest outlet to the Great Wall. We stopped to lunch at a village, and arrived in the evening at the old town. It is at the foot of a mountain pass, fifteen miles in length between mountains of very considerable height. The wall here is not in good preservation, and did not impress me with the awe which I knew I ought to feel at this great work. It (the Wall) comes down from the hills in a steep incline across the foot of the pass, and the gate in it is at once the frontier outlet and the gate of the town. We arrived at a tolerable inn, where we passed a good night. Farquhar's boy is a capital cook, and here, and indeed everywhere, turned us out a good meal. We set off up the pass the next morning on foot, as the road is so bad that mules can scarcely keep their footing. Carts would be dashed to pieces on it. The macadamizing process has not been put in force here, and the paving of the [track] is composed of huge boulders that have fallen from the hills on either side. How the animals ever got to the top still seems a mystery; but get to it they did, at the middle of the day. We lunched at a road-side inn, and in the evening arrived at a tolerably large walled town. Now as the inns are all the same and the accommodation varies but little, I shall beg you to take for granted, that we reached some one place or other every night. The next four days' journey was through level cultivated land; and from the absence of scenery and incident, was monotonous. On the fifth, being about 100 miles from the capital we fell in with a French Missionary, Père David,[1] whose name is well known at home in connexion with natural history. He was on a visit to some of his brethren in the north, to whom he gave us a letter of introduction. He had left that day a town called *Hsuan-hiva-fu* which he described as being in great confusion. The chief officer of the frontier troops had committed suicide rather than bear the remonstrances of his men, grumbling because their pay had not been sent up from Peking. We were cautioned to look well to our luggage, for the disbanded soldiers were wandering about the country.—Nothing occurred however. At this town we were subjects of immense curiosity to the natives who rarely see foreigners pass that way. The French Missionaries all adopt the Chinese dress, and conform as much as possible to Chinese manners. We called on the gentlemen, and saw two of them who told us that if we would stay a day there they could give us some good shooting. We did so and next day bagged a great number

---

1 Père Jean Pierre Armand David, 1826–1900, pioneer plant collector and naturalist in China from 1860 to 1874.

of duck and widgeon. My gun acts worthy of all Mr Braddell's commendations. Nothing of any consequence occurred till we arrived at Kal-gau (called by the Chinese *Chang-chia-K'ow*), the large frontier town on the borders of Mongolia.

Here we found all the inns full of soldiers on their way to the west provinces to quell some rows that the Mahometans were making there.—After much difficulty we got rooms in a miserable place outside the wall—and when the mules were unpacked sent our passport up to the Mandarin for inspection. It came back stamped and next morning we started up another tremendous pass. We were nearly all day getting to the top of it and at last just as the sun set we arrived on the great plateau. For miles and miles, nothing but one unbroken level was to be seen—but for the absence of grass (which is usually supposed to luxuriate in such places) it might be called a *"paraira!"* A cold wind now came on to blow, and we were glad to take to greatcoats and mufflers which we had not yet worn. We got that night to a lonely house on the plain (or rather plateau), the only Mansion in sight, where we found an interesting family of Mongolians, at their evening meal. They were glad to see [us], and turned out of their places to accommodate us. Fortunately there were more rooms than one, and we got a room to eat in and sleep in. The true Mongol is about the dirtiest person on the face of the earth. He displays however a taste for dress which shews itself by adopting gaudy colours. Yellow and bright red are the chief ones.

In appearance they are below the middle height, strongly made with broad laughing faces—a contrast to the suspicious looks and downcast eyes of the majority of the Chinese. In this place (and as we went farther it was *worse*), their curiosity was unbounded. Our clothes were examined (some of them tried on); watches, boots, whips, caps, and everything about us scrutinized and fairly remarked upon. The women are not so closely kept as the Chinese but yet do not mix freely with strangers; and for that, thank goodness! If they are so dirty or smell so offensively as the men, the less of them the better. Some of the people we met spoke Chinese; the best of them about as well as myself! Some of them much worse; but these were the most northerly whom we visited. Next morning our first day's journey in Mongol-land was a very inauspicious beginning: the wind was right in our teeth, and blowing half a gale. Nothing but hard walking enabled us to keep heat in our bones. That, travelling at a foot-pace, day after day over ground exactly the same, soon became monotonous. Except when a deer crossed our path, there was no excitement. Our next stage was Erh-Tái, which means the second military station (of the Chinese in Mongolia). They go on at regular intervals to Kiachta, a Russian town, on the frontier of Siberia. The officers and troops stationed at them, are both Mongolian. At this place, Farquhar tried to buy ponies, but not finding one that could beat his own, he did not come to terms. Immense herds of ponies, cattle and sheep form the entire produce of these people. *They are not allowed to cultivate the land under pain of death*! (at these stations, I mean), and we saw no other habitations.

The consequence was that we saw nothing like a flower garden till we again came down near the wall.—Everywhere here we experienced the best treatment possible. And it was not till we came down to the Chinese inns that we again met with obtrusive familiarity. Wanton incivility is totally unknown to either tribe. I need not describe to you each day's journey over the prairie, for one differed nothing from another. We travelled there a fortnight, going northeast a good way, and then south. We saw immense eagles, ravens, foxes and hares together with a small species of antelope, called *huang-yang* (yellow-sheep) in colour and size like a chamois, with short curved horns. Immense numbers of them are sent down to the Chinese game-markets and we have them from November till March. I fired at them; but without success. I am no *dab* at rifle-shooting; and my companions were no more fortunate. Well the end of all this was that we got down from the table land on the 15th day after we arrived on it, by another pass which it took us three days to get down. The roads however were good; (it had more roads than one); and the scenery was magnificent. We were shut in by enormous hills the whole time: and often as we wound round a turn, we had a glorious view of hill tops for miles and miles around us, and below us. Nothing but hill tops was to be seen, but when the setting or the rising sun shone on them they were worth looking at. On the evening of the third day we came to Kú-pei-K'ow (the old northern pass, same as *pei* in *Pei-ching*, "the northern capital"). Here we saw the Great Wall in good preservation. It is not in itself an object of wonder, being not much higher than fifteen feet, nor wider than nine: but the way it is carried over the most break-neck precipices, in one unbroken line—and its enormous length entitle it—I think—to be called the greatest work of human labour. The inside of it is often no higher than six feet but the outside is on the top of places where there is not as much room—supposing one could climb to it—as would serve to plant a scaling ladder. it is all faced with bricks, of such durability that the masonry is still intact; but the heart is filled with rubble and composite; the weight of which, I have no doubt, has caused the masonry to fall out in many places. I brought away a stone and a piece of mortar from it as a trophy. We slept in the little town there that night; and having seen the wall the next morning started at noon for Peking, where we arrived the next evening.

I could tell you of many amusing things that occurred, but my time is limited by the calls of business. And in reality there was not much out of the way. McKean kept the purse and regulated our expenditure while on the journey: and as he was determined not to be "done" by the innkeepers, we had some squabbling occasionally, in which the inn-keeper, from his superior knowledge of the Chinese tongue, *generally* had the best of the argument. At these inns too, a custom obtained of poking holes in the paper of the windows to watch the domestic habits of the distinguished foreigners. Eating or drinking, going to bed or rising up you were always sure to find an evil eye peeping at you. We got used to it at last, and never complained, unless there were more than *six* at a time! After all we had a very jolly trip of it, and I was sorry to get back again to work.

January 12th 1867—I have rewritten the above this evening from sundry notes and scraps of paper which I had. I might have spun it out: but I thought that what I have said was quite as much as your patience would endure.

I got your letters of the 19th of October yesterday. They came overland by camels from Chefou, as the river now is quite hard progress. This goes by the same way, and will not reach you for nearly three months. I am very sorry to hear of poor Aunt Finlay's sufferings, and I am glad that you have send her round to Janet to nurse. You have had enough of nursing of late; first Andrew and then Bella. The rest of you all seem to be well. Thank Maggy for her "racy" letter. I knew she would be sorry to leave school when the time came. Let us hope she has improved by it. Nothing new since I wrote the other day. I have had a headache, and a pain in the eyes, which the Doctor says is from reading too late at night by candle-delight. Do not imagine that I am working too hard. Nothing of the kind. You know *that* at least is none of my failings! But I took my recreation in the day time for some time, intending to make up for it at night—but I find it won't do: so I rise now an hour earlier, and have my exercise and work both in the day light. In everything else I am perfectly well.

We have now eight students in all. One of them is a retired lieutenant who resigned his commission to come with "us!" They are all very good fellows and we are very jolly.

We have now got our second rooms finished, and are much more comfortable than when we stuck in one room for reading and sleeping. Sir Rutherford Alcock who has our interest at heart has got us a great many improvements, and is trying to get us more.

I consider this letter as both to you and my father. Please tell him so, give him also my best love, and the same to the boys, and all the royal family and its offshoots: and with dearest love to yourself, I am, dear Mother,

Ever your loving son

To his Mother
British Legation—Peking, January 19th 1867

So short a time has elapsed between this letter and the sending off of the last that I have nothing new to tell you. The cold still continues intense and every drop of water exposed, is in a minute turned into ice. I enjoy the winter weather well enough, but I think on the whole the summer is preferable. We have already engaged a temple for the months.

A great many Europeans have come to Peking lately, as Professors to the Chinese school[1] in which European languages and sciences are taught. One of them, the Baron von Gumpach,[2] a German, is a great Hebrew scholar—knows my father's work on Textual Criticism, and says that when it came out, he was on the point of opening a correspondence with him.

He was delighted to read my father's reply to the Eclectic Reviewers which I lent him. He is a very nice gentleman indeed.

As I told you at the outset that there was nothing new, you will have been prepared for a sudden halt. Except to skate occasionally or to pay a visit or two, I am not often out of the Legation this weather. Work getting on tolerably but not very swiftly. I am likely to be sent off at the end of this summer to some place or other: which, all depends

1 The T'ung-wen Kuan or Interpreters' College was set up in 1862 to teach Chinese officials the languages needed to deal with the Western powers. To the English, French, German and Russian initially taught mathematics and astronomy were added in 1866. Hart was involved.
2 Count Johannes von Gumpach was appointed a professor in the college by Hart in 1866. It emerged that his real name was Theodor Gumpacht or Gumbracht and that he had been involved in some misdeed in 1843. He was dismissed by Hart in 1868.

on the amount of work to be done at the ports. If there is a press, they send up to Peking to ask for more hands. When you answer tell me all about Willy and his doings.

Love to my father, the boys and all, I am my dearest Mother,

Ever your loving son

To his Mother

British Legation—February 10th 1867

I was very glad to get your letter of November 17th which announced the arrival of my missing letters, for I was afraid that something had gone wrong with the Mail when I heard that you had not had any. If I had thought that my poor observations on the exercise I sent you, were to be submitted to so eminent a linguist as Dr MacDouall[1] I should have attempted something more scholarly. I could now give a much better opinion than then. Many thanks to you all for the care you are taking of my clothes and things. I am, thanks to you, getting on splendidly this cold weather. My vests and socks—and above all, the knitted waistcoat—are real blessings. The fine bright sunny days of last month, have given place to snowy and murky weather. There is no fog, or it would be a question whether I should cut my throat or hang myself from one of the beams of my room. This cannot however (the weather I mean) be of long continuance, for spring is fast coming on.

Peking and the Pekingese have both of them gone stark, staring, raving, howling mad. Last Tuesday the 4th February was their New Year's day. Now I am sure you have read in a good many books, of the festivities in which these wretched people indulge during that season: but no tongue nor pen can describe what has been going on here for the last ten days. Every house gives up its thousands of rockets and Roman candles, while the interval between these large fireworks is diversified by about a million of squibs. The most modest citizens beat gongs all night to the tune of the fireworks. For the first three nights sleep was a farce, and I lay awake speculating as to whether the next report would be that of a sky-rocket or a Devil's finger, as I think they call that small piece of ordnance, about a foot long which goes off in a series of deafening cracks at intervals of about ten seconds. The streets on the eve of the New Year were very gay; every house had ten

1 Charles MacDouall, LL.D., D.Lit., professor of Latin, 1849–50, professor of Greek, 1850–78 in Queen's College, Belfast.

or twelve lanterns in front of it, and the effect was very good. But, dear! while you were walking along, gazing at this fine sight, you found yourself in a hole in the street almost fit to bury you in. I went into a temple, and saw some of the "joss-pigeon" going on but was not much affected by anything I saw. In three days more, comes on the famous feast of lanterns (not the "feast of roses") when the cannonading will recommence, and my peace of mind will vanish.—Our teachers get a fortnight's holyday at this time, and I can do nothing but make up back-work; but the rest is a good thing too, even if no work were done. By the way, a singular fatality has attended all my teachers. My first died. A man who came to do his business while he was sick, also died with two of his children and his wife; and my present "*bloke*" has just lost a child, after the death of his wife some weeks ago. I cannot lay the flattering unction to my soul that I worked the men to death; besides that would not account for the children. But the fact is unimpeachable.

I shall tell you a few particulars about an execution which I was foolish enough to see (for I lost a night or two sleep by it) in my next letter. This one is already too long.

No more news of Willie, as I see by your not mentioning him at all in your letter. I have written to him pretty much in the same strain as I wrote to you, and advised him to think well before attempting any change. Though advice from me is not I think likely to weigh much with him. You will let me hear of any thing that he contemplates.

My *Whigs* have not come regularly the last two Mails, but this is on account of the out of the way method of getting the Mails up here. I have got one of *each* Mail; but there are two still on their way. The bags are opened at Shanghai, and a certain weight is sent one *way*, and the rest by the other. The two ways, are "[1]direct overland from Chin Kiang, and [2]round to Chefoo by steamer, and thence overland to Peking", so they will come soon I make no doubt. I was anxious to read about that madman McMechan's meetings. I hope my father will process Harper for the damages and get them too: the old *rogue*! I see by some of the English papers that the floods in Belfast have been enormous. You told me about Bella's house being flooded. I hope that no damage was done, and that they have got back into it again. My news conveniently was at the foot of a page; and as I have no more to say—not even old twaddle I stop. So good bye: and believe that I am as Ever, dearest mother,

Your loving son

To his Mother

British Legation, Peking—March 13th 1867

"Predestination is the thief of time" as we know, and I have predesti-
nated to such an extent since the departure of the *last* Mail that I have
left little or no time for anything by *this*. Nothing however of any
interest has occurred here, and this may console you for a short letter.
Your last letters bore date of the 2nd of January, I think, and were very
pleasant indeed. I am glad that Johnny got over to see you all. You
make a *tower* some day to see him. I am looking out anxiously for the
arrival of my box which will come up I think by our new doctor who
comes out by the same Mail. I shall let you know the moment it arrives.
My *Whigs* come regularly now two by every Mail. Belfast seems to be
wonderfully quiet now, by the absence of news in the papers. Those
brutes have got their New Year's festivities at last over and order and
harmony again prevail. The weather grows warmer every day; in
another month it will be uncomfortably so. I cannot write to any body
else this time: but I promise you a good long letter next fortnight, come
what will. My last two months' letters have not been, I know, what they
should have been; but better write nothing at all than either fill a letter
with nonsense or lies; and beyond these there is nothing at all. With
love to my father and all, I am as ever,

Your loving son

To his Mother

British Legation, Peking—March 27th 1867

I shall try by this Mail to let you have a longer letter than usual though
where I am to get news to put into it, I cannot at present tell. I may get
inspiration as I go on. Your letters of the last Mail in January arrived
here the other day. I was terribly surprised to hear of Sandy's misfortune. It was about the last thing in the world I should have thought of.
He will, however, I have no doubt get his head above water in another
year, and in the meantime, he has those other branches of his business
to keep him going. The next most important event was the despatching
of my box. It has not yet arrived and I am looking anxiously for it every
day. A box of McKean's which came probably by the same Mail has

not arrived either. I expect our new doctor Powles will bring them both up from Shanghai. I should have sent you home some more money and indeed I have some few dollars laid up: but I find it hard to increase the heap, for this is no place for saving, though one would say there were not many opportunities of spending. But don't be uneasy; sooner or later—(chiefly sooner)—you shall have all I can manage to send. Your Belfast frost of a fortnight seems a most contemptible affair after Peking; though indeed the ice here was not enjoyable after a fortnight; for the dust got into the ice; and except in one or two places, such at the lake at the Summer palace, skating was impossible. The March winds are as boisterous and unpleasant here as at home—and having more dust to play with, make walking intolerable. Dust storms have been raging for the last fortnight, at intervals of one or two days.—Our races have come and gone. I bought a pony very cheap; and after a little training he turned out a first rate little fellow. He won two races and ran third for another, so that he paid his expenses; and I have him still to sell or do what I like with. I am detailing to James the amount of the whole affair, and he will tell you all about it. I wish my riding toggery had come out in time but I borrowed a pair of top boots—and a China man built me a pair of breeches of some kind of drab stuff which *looked* well, though I cannot say so much for their wearing qualities.

The Legation is dull; and though we have (at least the chief has) another noble duke of the exiled family of Louis Philippe; in point of fact, a grandson of that old swaddler, I forget his name; but he is in the American navy, and speaks English with the peculiar intonation of that country. They (i.e. he and a count somebody of somewhere) have gone to the Great Wall for a trip. Beyond their arrival, nothing since the races has given rise to any interest.

At this period of my letter, I am obliged to confess that I have nothing to say. To ask questions would only be [to] enrage you, and I have no other resource but to close up my budget. I am well and strong; and getting on at the lingo as hard as I can. I shall answer my father's letter by next Mail. *Northern Whigs* and *Christian Unitarians* are pouring in regularly every Mail. Love to all, not forgetting Maggie: to whom I owe several long essays; and with dear love to yourself I am ever,

Your loving son

To his Mother

British Legation, Peking—April 9th 1867

Your letters written on receipt of my short note of November last year
came safely to hand the other day. I am afraid you will think me lazy
in respect of writing to you and my last few letters surely justify you
but in the absence of interesting news what can a man do? It is only
now and then that anything worth telling you about occurs and when
it does I always communicate it, and a good deal more I am afraid. My
box has not yet arrived but neither has the doctor, and I expect them
both together. I shall [at] once relieve your minds by letting you hear
of the event. Nothing new in your letters, to answer or comment upon
though your accounts of all at home are very pleasant. Maggie's return
will doubtless make a great difference to you in the house, chiefly in
the evenings, now that two more cock-chickens have wandered from
the nest, Johnnie and myself: but with James, Drummond and Polly
you ought to have a jolly enough house. Thank James and Polly for
their letters. I shall perhaps answer one of them by this Mail. I see you
were anticipating some amusement from my account of my Mongolian
expedition and I may be able to afford you some soon though the short
scrawl I did send home merely told you where I was without details.
I shall write up a short diary; (indeed I am half through it already); and
send it home to you for private perusal—remember no handing about
to Faimoran or printing in periodicals. The latter course would be down
rightly injurious to me, as it would be at once known from whose pen
it came (for there were two men with me who would at once recognise
the narratives) and writing to public prints is as much as possible
discountenanced in the service, for fear some one might write *too
much*. So much for Buckingham! I shall not commence writing so
soon; *thank you*!

I hope that the Kaffir Chieftains[1] may come home for good to stay
with you and soon. My father would never want company as long as
Uncle William was with him. This seems rather a truism, like saying
that a man will never be blind so long as he sees: but you know what
I mean even though the mumping be ever so indistinct. And as long as
Mr Lynar could get up an argument upon such a topic as the proper
way to jump off a hack-car in motion, as I remember he did once at

1 Hon. William Porter retired from the attorney generalship at the Cape in 1865. He
  returned to live with his brother in 1873 after the death of his friend Hugh Lynar.

breakfast. Having disposed of you all by this time, let me say a word of myself and my doings. I am *of course* well, and of course busy. Beyond this I have not much to say. The Legation is full of visitors from the south of China. The Duke, or rather Duc de Penthièvre has gone away again with his suite, and has been succeeded by a Major Crossman, Superintendent of Consular buildings in China; a Mr Gibb, of Gibb, Livingstone and Co. Ship-owners, and several more whose names I do not remember. Five new students are expected in another month, having left England in the end of March. No friends of mine among them. They are to be bundled off to a distant temple the moment they arrive, and kept there till new houses are built for them. Some unhappy student will be told off to look after them, and do any negotiations that may take place between them and the Chinese. I pray heartily for exemption. I am not going to a temple this year unless I find that I am totally unable to stay in the city, and even then, not till the summer is far advanced. I am comfortably settled now, and dread any change. The weather is very changeable just now, and if one is not cautious, colds are inevitable. Dust reigns supreme and nobody thinks of stirring out of the Legation. My work is going on well now, and I can speak with a fair average fluency as regards common topics of conversation, though I have technical terms to make up before I can call my knowledge general. If I am not sent away for another year, I will be of some use to old Victoria yet. Sir Rutherford wants to keep us here as long as he can; but at a pinch he must send some one away. If I could get a chance of sending my father the books I have for him, I should be very glad, but none such appears likely to turn up. The first chance I get I shall send them and a few other little things.

Having heard that an execution of criminals was going to take place some time ago, I went to see it; not so much through idle curiosity, as a desire to see how the Chinese manage such things. The execution grounds is simply a street, at the part of it where another large street runs into it. On this street were erected two matting sheds, on opposite sides of it and facing one another. The one was closed in front, and was for the criminals while waiting their turn to be executed; the other was open in front and was for the officials who were conducting the execution. We went down about eight o'clock in the morning and found a great crowd, and the street blocked up on both sides of these temporary houses. We had no difficulty in getting inside however; and as soon as we got in bargained with a shopkeeper to let us go on the roof of his house, to see all that was to be seen. This done, we went and saw the criminals, who were as lively as possible, apparently careless of the fate that awaited them. They were about fifteen in number, one of whom was a woman. They were not chained up or confined in any way, except that their hands were tied behind their backs. An arrow was fixed at their backs, sticking up about two feet above their heads, and pasted on the top of this was the name, the crime and the sentence of the unfortunate wretch. One man had cut his father's throat while shaving the old gentleman one morning. He was beheaded. Most of the others were highway robbers and kidnappers. The woman was of the latter class. Notwithstanding their condition, our appearance was the signal for a burst of levity! They examined us as minutely and as curiously, and were altogether as jolly as if they had been going to a fête, and one or two of them, who said they had known foreigners, asked for foreign cigars; and this from men who knew that in half an hour they would be dead. Farther down the street was a small sentry box in which the swords were deposited for the time, watched over by two attendants. They are all of great antiquity; and all have names and *official rank*! On the handles are carved hideous likenesses of men's heads. The sword to be used that day was about two feet long in the blade; the blade was about three inches deep and the back of it about an inch in breadth so as to give great weight to the blow. They were kept in wooden scabbards, covered with yellow silk, the imperial colours. The officials then began to arrive, and soon afterwards the imperial order for the execution was brought down by a very high Mandarin on horseback gorgeously dressed with a numerous suite of attendants. The other officials were also in full dress. After some confabulation, they all ranged themselves at a table in the tent, looking out to the street. The first victim was then brought out and forced to kneel before them, while his sentence was read to him. At the conclusion of it, he knocked his head to the ground; and was then taken down by the police about seventy yards further down the street, where the executioner was waiting for him. This official was not looked upon by the crowd as Calcraft is at home—nor was there anything repulsive in his appearance. He was dressed just as any other man, with the exception of the official hat, and a yellow apron that had marks of previous slaughter. The victim was forced into a kneeling posture on the street (none of your gallows and scaffold!) so as to keep his head up, or rather *out* the ends of the cord were twined into the pigtail, which was grasped by the assistant butcher, and the man's head was thus stretched out so as to give a fair blow at the neck. A man sat on his feet and kept him from being pulled too far forward. The executioner advanced sword in hand, rolled up his sleeves, and tried the weapon

7 An execution scene, *c.*1860: photographer unknown

by shaking it in the air; he then put it about half a foot above the neck, raised it slowly till about level with his own head, and shouting quickly "Don't stir", came down full on the neck. There was a dull sound, and the head was off. The assistant who was holding the pigtail almost fell when he no longer found any resistance to his pull. The crown cried "*hae tao*", "*hao ta*!" ("Good sword, good stroke!") and the execu-tioner carried the bloody head to the mandarins, after shewing it to whom, he flung it beside the body. The rest of the malefactors were strangled; an operation which was performed by some whip-cord and a short piece of stick, which was inserted in the cord and twisted round till the man died. After seeing one specimen of each system, we came away—sadder and wiser men. I dreamed of the thing for a considerable number of nights; but have now got over that weakness. I don't suppose you take much interest about such things but my father or the boys may be anxious to know how the criminals are "turned off" (as Mr Dennis says) in Peking. So little is known about China at home, that almost anything is acceptable; though you may say the less known about such things the better. I must now conclude. Please remember me to all at home and elsewhere. Tell everybody to expect long letters from me soon! And now I must dry up for nothing else comes into my head. With best love to yourself, I am dearest mother

Ever your loving son

P.S.—*Weekly Whigs* and occasionally *Newsletters* pour in with the utmost regularity, I miss the light reading of the *Christian Unitarian*.

To his Mother

British Legation, Peking—April 25th 1867

The last letters that came from you bore date of the end of February, and came about four days ago. Neither from them nor the papers could I find that anything new was going on. You had not got my expected notes on Mongolian experiences and would no doubt be greatly disappointed at the summary way in which such an interesting topic was dismissed in the letter which [you] have got by this time. But I shall send you the original *some day soon*! My box has not arrived yet; but the long expected Doctor is at Tientsing and I may expect it every day. If he does not bring it I shall feign illness, at least twice a day, and consume all his medicines just to spite him.

It is pleasant in the midst of the cares of business to hear such good accounts of everyone at home, and to find that they have not forgotten to write me a line or two occasionally. I would answer them by every Mail; but I have told you often and often, I have not what fills up one letter, and therefore cannot write more. I write to James by this Mail, and shall manage, I hope, to pay off Johnny and Maggy by the next. I am very glad that Andrew is so busy and hope he may continue to be so for a long time. If I had intended I could not go to the hills this summer, for I am doing work in the Chancery with the two Secretaries, which will oblige me to be here the whole time. It does not take up much of my time; and as I shall be engaged on work of a similar kind at any consulate, as well as at interpreter's duty, I am now getting into the way of it. *Weekly Whig* still comes regularly. Our new students are soon to be here; and the Legation, at least our end of it, is in a horrid state of dirt with builders putting up quarters for them. Indeed there has been building and repairing ever since I came here. I shall try and make a longer letter next time: till then I am,

Ever your loving son

To his Mother

Peking—May 8th 1867

I have to answer only one letter (no *two*) of yours by the last Mail dated,
I think the end of February. I hope the boys are not disgusted with me
for not writing to them—however by this Mail I write to Johnny and I
hope soon to work off any disagreeable impressions on their part.
There was not much news in the last arrivals from you, though to hear
that you were all so well was news enough. My "Essays" to Maggie
in reply to her admirable "papers" are in course of composition: tell
her so. I am glad to hear that Bella is getting strong again, and that the
dear wee nieces and nephews are all so well. Holywood would have
been a nice place for them all; the young ones particularly; I doubt if
they find Green island so pleasant. I can understand Andrew's idea of
lodging in Miss Whittle's[1] during the Assizes and surely you have him
near enough to you there, besides having attorneys' clerks to wipe their
feet on your carpet.

And now my box has at last arrived! laden with all the products of
your western looms. The oil-cloth round the things was a good idea;
for after serving as an impervious cover to my clothes, it now is
converted into a table cover! and an excellent one it makes barring that
it is a little frayed at some of the corners. All the things fit well, except
the coats made by that prince of tailors Arnold. He must have a very
exalted idea of the height of my person, for his coats are made for a
giant of seven feet or more. The other things all suit admirably,
particularly those made by McCullough who really makes *well*.
McCullum's coats fit so nicely that after taking an hour to pull on, I
was obliged to pass the night in them! (*fact*!!!). They are however a
little easier now. The songs are good and many thanks for them, as well
as for the pictures which already adorn my walls. The men here won't
believe that I crossed the bridge at Carrick a Rede:[2] and I am looked
upon as little less than a lunatic for saying that my father and sister
both accomplished the feat. It certainly looks worse in the picture than
it is in reality—though bad enough in either. James no doubt well
remembers the day when he and I crossed it in presence of a troup of
ladies, who absolutely shrieked to see two such fine fellows hurrying
as they thought to certain and inevitable ruin.

---

1 The Misses Whittle conducted a boarding school at 1 Fisherwick Place, adjacent
   to the Porter home.
2 Then, as now, a tourist attraction on the north Antrim coast.

To accommodate Sir Rutherford (and indeed myself too) I am now staying at a temple just outside the western wall of the city, called *Tien ling ssŭ*, The old chief is gone down south on an excursion to the consulates at the different ports, to see the state of affairs at each, as several rather nasty little things have turned up which render supervision occasionally necessary. Having taken rooms in this temple (which is a very large one, and from its proximity to the Legation very convenient) that he might occasionally come out, he wanted someone to occupy them while he was away, that on his return he might not find himself dispossessed, and two of us were asked to come out if we liked. I was very glad for this is the pleasantest time of the year; not *too* hot— though the sun at noon-day is strong enough. I ride in every day— or second day, for I have not yet sold my pony. I shall try to dispose of him when I leave the temple, as I don't want riding in the summer.

The building is still going on in the Legation, and indeed is likely to go on for ever. Since I came they have been in a constant state of tearing down, building up, plastering, hammering and all the other adjuncts of repairing on a large scale. Our quarters are to form a quadrangle by themselves at the north end; of which the mess-room, and a house at each end of it for Murray and Brown will form one side. The present row of modern-looking cottages as Mrs Lieut Colonel Muter in her *Notes on China* calls our diggings, will stand, as it does now, facing the mess-room, and two new sides will be built. I am glad to be out of the way of all the dirt and din, you may imagine.

Weekly Whigs as regular as if I were at Larne, not Peking. It was quite time the *Christian Unitarian* was stopped, for the matter of it was getting less interesting while the vituperation was much more feeble than in its palmiest days. The Congregational Memoirs are sorry stuff to read through; and indeed I suppose no one did read them. I hope the Fenians before this have got a good lesson from the "*sojers*"—and that numbers of them have been hanged (!!!) I am almost afraid to appear in my big boots, for fear I should be taken for "a brother" after Drummond's description of them, as "fellows in green uniform, with big top boots!" I naturally avoid carefully any garments of a verdant hue, as suspicion would, if I donned them, be too strong.

I am working in the Chancery at present; and am likely to be there all summer, or indeed till I go away from Peking, and my time is not so much at my disposal as before, though nothing to interfere with my study. There will probably be a clearance made when the chief comes back from the southern posts and I may be packed out then. Eighteen months here is looked upon as about the fair time for a man to study though two years is the normal time. Love to all. I am writing to Johnny and shall send my own recognitions.

Ever your loving son,

To his Mother
British Legation, Peking—May 28th 1867

I have not much to reply to in your letters of the last Mail which duly arrived here after a voyage or passage of only 50 or 51 days, the fastest that I have seen here. I am glad to see that you are all in good spirits, even with the Fenians at your door; for I see by the *Whig* that numerous captures of the brethren have been effected in Belfast. And let me here state that the *Whig* comes with the most unerring punctuality. Summer has at last (for I told you that the spring days here are very changeable) come in—hot strong and plenty of it. I have been obliged to leave my temple on account of the heat; for business compelled me to come in three or four times a week, and I feared the strong sun. The Chinamen begin now to go about with hats to keep the head cool, at a time when we are all wearing helmets to keep the sun off. But this is by no means the greatest of their peculiarities. I think I told you that just when the sun begins to grow hot, they open up the sewers in the city. What can be done with people like this?

Two things out of the ordinary run have occurred:— One the arrival of five new students, and the other the death of Sir Eric Farquhar, whom you already know as my companion in Mongolia. He had gone down to Tientsin to see the races there, and on coming back took ill, and was dead in ten days. Typhus fever was the cause. His death has caused a deep gloom to fall upon our small community, for nobody was more beloved than he. He had been left in charge of the Legation while the chief was away, and was going home as soon as the latter came back. He had been transferred to Stockholm. His funeral was attended by everybody in Peking. The cemetery is about six miles from the Legation, under the west wall of the city; too far to walk in a boiling sun, though we started at six in the morning. Six Escort men, mounted and in full uniform attended the coffin, two before and four behind. We rode behind them. It is not known yet whether his friends will have his remains sent home: most probably they will.

The other event is a more pleasant one. We now make a mess of thirteen and another man is soon coming up which will relieve the squeamish of the party of the necessity of sitting down with so unlucky a number. I don't mind for myself. The names of the five new men are Margary, Giles, Abdy, Warren (the son of an Admiral) and Scott: *all* Englishmen. At first the Scotch had the ascendancy; then the mess was almost exclusively Irish; and now by this influx of the Sassenach, English is the order of the day. By the way, the man who came next to me when I was examined (only twelve months behind, I think) has since had his heart's desire fulfilled and is now out with us. Two other men, Margary and Scott, were each up four times in all, and were also up in my year! Oxenham is the man who came so near me.

When you get a chance of any college news or any news of any of my friends, you will let me hear about them. I still take an interest in such things. Tell my father that neither the speeches on the Education Question, nor the gallant Colonel's poetical effusions have come out yet—but will of course come by the first man that comes out to his post. They must have been too late for these men to bring. I read a review of "Mount Carmel" or "Calvary" or whatever he calls it, in which the work was not thought or made much of. I expect great amusement from it.

The painters and paper-hangers are in my room now; and the smell of the paint in this hot weather, has driven me to work in the Library for some days. I have tried the old dodge of putting a tub full of water in the room, to absorb the effluvium of the paint, but without success. I know of no other remedy but patience and that is none at all. The work is getting on fast though: and the paint dries so quickly here that soon it will be all right again. My work is getting on well; and I find that by regular habits of study one comes at last to be scarcely able to *idle*. I work regularly about nine hours a day: never less than eight—I cannot keep my thoughts on the stretch longer: but I do a good deal in the time. Besides I am paid by old Victoria to work all my time and do nothing else, and I *ought* to work that much. The laborious part of it too is now diminished by increased knowledge of the spoken language, and explanations from the teacher are no longer incomprehensible.

My news at this point has failed me and I can no longer go on. I shall continue to write to you by every Mail and tell you *all I know*. I should write separately to my father: but I consider letters to you as also to him. When I have enough to make two I shall also write to him. Love to all: not forgetting Andrew: and with earnest love to yourself, I am dearest Mother,

Ever your loving son

To his Mother
June 15th 1867

No letters came from you by the last Mail—the first time that I have missed any budget since I left home. I am quite sure however that you sent them, and that something occurred to detain them. Probably Drummond who was despatched to post them carried them about in his pocket, for a week or so! (Look hard at him, while you read this in a severe voice). But my papers came, and one or two odd ones too from James: one of which contained an account of the "Varsity boat-race". I see by the *Whigs* that Andrew is getting a large share of business, and that's a satisfactory thing. Have you heard anything of the other exile lately? Has he married yet? I wrote to him but have had no answer for if he cannot find time to write often to you, he cannot manage a line to me. I shall write on till I get one at all events. Everything here is dull. The Chief is still in the south and is not expected back for some time yet. A new Secretary, by name of Frazer has come. He was to have taken poor Farquhar's place. I am in good health as usual. I may expect to be sent away this autumn to a moral certainty; for when the chief comes back he will no doubt despatch men down to ports to supply vacancies, and indeed I shall not be sorry for a little change. Not that I don't like this place, but I should prefer being near the sea, especially in the summer time. The dust here is *the* drawback, and while I am writing it is flying in clouds as thick as a London fog: (which I never saw!) The society here is of course much better than at any other place in China: and good society makes up even for excessive dust.

I am almost run out: but I shall send you another letter in a few days by the Russian Mail, and you can test the comparative speed of the two modes of conveyance.

Ever, dearest Mother, your loving son

To his Mother
British Legation, Peking—July 5th 1867

I have a great many letters of yours to answer, for as I told you in my last, one of your Mails was late, and came to me with the following one, both together. I wrote to you, through Russia by the last (or at the time the last Mail was going) and had the intention of writing by both; but I found that I was repeating in the one exactly what I had said in the other, and that would not interest you, you know. The chief point of interest [in your letters] was Willy's marriage. But what made *you* go to the trouble of copying out his long letter? James I am sure would have done so. Many thanks for it though. He seems at last to be nearer comfort and happiness than he has been since he left Uncle William's house in Cape Town. I don't believe he will turn Roman Catholic; for if he takes any interest in matters of that kind, he has sense enough for the rest.[1] I have written to him and mean to do so again. I am very very sorry to hear about Sandy's misfortune, and the illiberal and ungenerous way he has been treated by his creditors. I hope that Bella is keeping up through it all. Better times are in store for them and for us all.

It seems scarcely more than the other day that I was writing to you, muffled up in coats and sitting at a blazing fire, and now, lo, all is changed. Peking for the time being, is converted into an oven, which resembles as much as anything can, the dry stifling heat of the place. Now and then, the scene is diversified by crashes of thunder that shake the house, after which floods of rain fall; but the ground is so deplorably dry that a fortnight's rain would be all swallowed up, and yet no perceptible coolness. The long continued dry weather of the two previous months and the absence of much snow in the winter have proved the destruction of the first crops and a famine is apprehended. It may be averted however by the occasional rains of this month, if the people have their second crop in. All round the city stealing and open robbery are among the results of this drought and dearth. My teacher tells me that an insurrection is feared, and that the Emperor is laying in stores of rice to give to the distressed. Will he ever do so? *Credat Judæus Apella; non ego!* (I quote to an accomplished scholar.) Talking of the thunder shaking the house—we had an earthquake the other day—think of that Mrs P! a good *bona fide* earthquake. I had gone to bed shortly after eleven, and was not yet asleep, when I felt the room slightly tremble, and then shake violently while the windows rattled like fury. The man who sleeps in the same house jumped up, rushed in to me, and proposed that we should go out and about all night away from the houses: which he felt certain were about to fall, "dragging down a mighty ruin". But I lay on and saw it out. There was another slight tremble, and after that no more. So there is another experience I have passed through.

1 He married Margaret Carroll in St Augustine's Roman Catholic Church on 4 March 1867.

The chief came back the other day from his tour to the south, looking much stronger and less paralytic than before his departure. The only news of interest to you about his visit and its results, is that new men are to go down in October, of whom I am pretty sure to be one. An examination will be held before anything is done, and I am not afraid of passing creditably. I don't care now whether I go down or not: for one can after being a year and more in Peking continue Chinese studies anywhere, even in Belfast. I wish they would establish a consulate there and send me.

The Alcock family has gone to its temple: rather late in the season when we have only another month of heat. I am thinking of going in September when the evenings and mornings are cooler, and the ephemeral (no: not *ephemeral*; perhaps perennial?) sandflies and mosquitos are dead, and life becomes again supportable. No matter how coarse the bait—Chinamen or European—their motto is *"Tras Tyriusve mihi nullo discrimine agetur!"*[1] (More Latin! I am growing pedantic. Thank Goodness, other plagues of the night, such as the *cimex vulgaris* are not rife here—or suicide must follow.

From Drummond's letters to you, he seems to be or to have been, enjoying himself in Dublin. I know I did when I was there; but then I was older. It is a good idea certainly, Drummond taking Andrew here and there, as Andrew calls it. Please tell the former gentleman that his last letter to me, which consisted of a series of fragments among which a card containing an advertisement in verse from some enterprising cobbler, was *not* the least remarkable, came to fearful grief on the road out. Mr Wade opened the bag at Shanghai for his own letters, kindly collected the fragments, but put them all into a strong envelope and sent them on to me. But it is not pleasant for one to have things like that made public. Other people only laugh at what, though they may have value for us appear ridiculous to them. So in future tell him to send his communications, especially those containing cards (which readily cut through covers) in strong envelopes. And indeed you might all bear that in mind. Several of my letters have had the covers rubbed off; though hitherto the contents were not of such a motley description as in this last case. Besides no object is gained, no purpose is served, and no expense is saved by thin envelopes.

I had much more news (if news it can be called that news is none) in my head when I sat down—but truly this process of conveying one's

---

1 Attorney General Porter used the same phrase, in English, about his attitude to the Boers in a speech in the legislative council in Cape town in 1852.

thought to paper, is calculated to drive even more than that out. I hope you came back from London, feeling better both in body and mind: though your stay there too, cannot but have been a little dull, Johnny being in at his work all day, and you being so far away from any friends. But change of any kind is an admirable thing. I quite forgot your birthday, my dearest mother, and indeed I am always content and even glad to forget all birthdays; for they only remind one that one is a year older; and that I think is best forgot. But I don't forget you. You will see I hope a good many birthdays before you see the birth of that day. The saving clause, I hope, might seem to imply the possibility that it might come. I merely meant that I hope you will see many more birthdays. Which subject brings me on to mention that one of the men called Giles is of the same year, month and day as I am viz 8th December. That's rather odd. Truly I had a narrow escape from being called Giles! Has James' disputed birthday ever been settled to his own satisfaction?

And now I must "dry up", as the Yankees say. Tell my father that money is not very plenty with me just now; and that though I may seem to be putting him off, it is in reality not so. I have a little by me, and in October, I can send something decent, when I get my extra pay. Meanwhile adieu! I shall write to my father by the Russian Mail of this week, to congratulate him upon a recent happy event in the Congregation; also to James. Love to Bella, Maggy and all. Ever My dearest Mother,

Your loving son

To his Mother

Peking—August 5th 1867

I have little to add to my last, and merely keep up the old arrangement of letting you know that I am still well and have been so since I wrote.

Your Mail of the end of May arrived here some days ago. You were at that time still in London. As you said in your letter that you were sure my father would give me all the home news, and he said just the same of you in his, I got no home news at all! But your letters are always good reading news or no news. I had a letter ready to send to my father via Russia, but on receipt of your Mail I postponed it. I have managed to get an order through a man here on the Hong Kong Bank, but as it has not come up to me yet, I cannot despatch it by this Mail. It will be about £22 or £23: I don't know the exact rate of the dollar, or I could tell you with certainty. It's all I can send at present though it is small enough. I shall write to my father when I remit the money. I hope you passed a pleasant time with your English friends, when on your way home to Belfast. I have no doubt the trip has done you good. It was provoking not to get the lodgings at Cushendall but I hope you have put upon some other place. A summer would not seem summer at all, without the sea-side. If I was inclined to forget that this was summer, I am unpleasantly reminded of the fact.

The heat is still very bad, though a shade less so in the morning and evenings than last month. The ice keeps us alive however. Poke people to write to me if you know any one likely to do so. I owe James scores of letters. Love to everyone and to yourself as much as you can take.

Your loving son

To his Mother
British Legation—September 7th 1867

I can only repeat what I am always repeating, that it would be idle to attempt to return you a like amount of news for what I receive from you. Your last long letter, written when you were just going to Ballantrae, was one of the pleasantest, most chatty (if one can use such a word of a letter) letters I have ever had from you, and of course from anyone. I hope—and indeed I am sure that you enjoyed yourselves at the sea-side. When the boys came down I am sure you did. I have, I think, a more vivid recollection of that place than of any other at which we stayed during the summers I was at home: I mean the whole place, not Ballantrae particularly. How I envy you the bathing and the water! It was a pity you could not get the old house; but I have no doubt you will make yourself comfortable in any locality.

I am very sorry to hear that Bella has been so poorly.—Sandy's affairs have no doubt contributed to that; and I trust that another Mail or two will bring better accounts of both. His creditors have dealt hardly with him indeed. My father mentions that he is uncertificated— which I presume is due to their obstinacy or his inability to satisfy

them. I suppose that you acted for the best in getting Drummond into
a merchant's house after all. It is singular that James and he and I
myself should never have had any decided taste for anything in
particular. Is it not? Johnny certainly had a leaning towards business.
Andrew chose his profession from the love of it. But I am out here
solely and simply because I was fit for nothing else, and did not want
to sit with my hands before me doing nothing any longer. I don't think
James has much taste for banking *as* banking. I may be wrong, and
hope I am. Not that he ever said word to me, to make me believe so;
but I think he was calculated to do much better. Now, of course, there
is nothing else for him; and if he sticks to it, he can shew ability there
as elsewhere. About Drummond perhaps I should not speak, as I have
not seen that distinguished member of the mercantile community since
he has begun to go on 'change: but when he was at school he appeared
to have no fixed idea of his future destiny. I am however quite satisfied
what chance has given me: so I hope is James: and Drummond will
probably be so as well. He will not of course go into office till you all
have come back from the shore. From the frequent appearance of his
name in the papers, I should say that Andrew must be getting on very
well indeed in his profession. No man deserves better to attain to the
highest honour, which his profession can give. I have never known
except in my father, more ability combined with application. I was
quite startled the other day on reading in Maggie's letter that he was
thirty years old. I had lost count of his age since he was seven and
twenty, and thought he was still that age. And I myself am nearly
twenty two! Gracious goodness! I shall be coming home for a wife
soon; so be on the look out, you and Bella.

The *Northern Whig* which still comes with unerring exactness
contained but little news this last time: but in some of the later papers,
I read the account of Maximilian's[1] murder (for I cannot but look upon
it as such) in Mexico. He met his death as a brave man should; and
despite his follies, that always will enlist sympathy. Like the Thane of
Cawdor—nothing in his life became him like the leaving of it. I don't
take a deep interest in European or any other politics; but I make it a
point to read the accounts from all the sources I can, of such things;
and keep up with the age.

I have written a business letter to my father; by which you will see
that I have sent twenty-five pounds to pay as many of the bills as that

---

1 The Austrian archduke installed as emperor of Mexico by the French and then
abandoned to his fate at the hands of Mexican revolutionists.

sum will cover for my last box. Next time I shall send the money with the order, and thus prevent any anxiety. The time is coming when I shall either be sent south, or kept here for another year: in either case on an increase of salary. This is pleasant: and sets my own mind comparatively at rest as to the sum I still owe my father. Be assured that whenever it is in my power I shall *pay up*. By steady reading, and no overwork, nor on the other hand any idleness, I have now made a fair progress in the Chinese language, chiefly the spoken; for which I find I am better adapted than many of the men around me. With this I am of use anywhere. A man who can read Confucius as you read Milton, is of no use if he cannot speak the colloquial. Of course the character must be attended to; but the speaking presupposes that; before you have attained any proficiency in it, you must also have read a good deal: for I believe a man cannot learn to speak Chinese unless he knows what he speaks by having first learned it in books; then practice with the natives does the rest. Don't imagine that I have done anything extraordinary, or that I [am] trying to make you believe I have. I only want you to know what I myself know to be the case. Hundreds of men are doing the same every day of their lives. No I am not given to boasting; for I know I have done nothing to boast of; but it is a sort of vindication from the charge of idleness; to which I was open when you last had the honour of my acquaintance.

The cool weather has come on now, and we are all once more enjoying existence; which we could scarcely be said to do a month ago. I stayed a fortnight at the hills, but was not very comfortable, and came away as soon as I could manage. I am conscious however that the short change of air was good for me, and I found the work got on much more briskly when I set to again.

Have you had any more news from Willy? I hope he and the mainspring get on well. But I need not ask you to tell me all about him or anything, for you always do that, my dear Mother.

If I could communicate as much pleasure to you by my letters, as you do to me by yours, I should be very proud indeed.

Love to all; Maggie included. Tell her I have not yet completed my celebrated Essay to her; but it is in course of preparation: and to yourself, the same old story—that I am, my darling mother,

Ever your loving son

To his Mother

British Legation, Peking—October 7th 1867

I have little more news to give you than that I received your letters and my father's of the end of July when you had just come back from the shore. I am very glad that you all enjoyed yourselves as much as you appear to have done. Maggie's bathing must be something quite uncommon to draw such a crowd of spectators. I did not imagine when she used to talk of being able to take six strokes, that she would ever really be able to swim in deep water. Johnny's usual bad luck in weather must have been a horrible thing for him, coming from such a distance. The only other news about "the royal family" that you letter contained, was that Andrew had gone to lodge near the Court-house, during the Assizes. It is very pleasant to hear that he has so much practice. I am sure he will get on well.

I am anxious to hear about the money order I sent in my last letter—if it arrived safely, and if the money was all right—though I have not much doubt on the latter score. I hope soon to be in a position to send you some more of the needful.

Of ourselves out here, little can be said. The chief and his party with Admiral Sir Henry Keppel have gone on a fortnight's trip to the Great Wall, and are expected back in a day or two. No else is new. Our examination which was to have been held three weeks ago has been postponed until they come back: as the old boy wishes to be present at the proceedings, though he does not know B from a bull's foot, as far as Chinese is concerned. His presence will only serve the purpose of frightening some of the fellows out of their wits. I really cannot think of anything more to tell you about: for nothing occurs here, and you already know the daily routine of a student in Peking. I am as always in good health and tolerable spirits, and that is always good. I am glad to see from your note that you are so too. My next letter shall be longer.

Love to my father and to all the rest: and believe that I am ever, dearest Mother,

Your loving son

To his Mother
British Legation—November 5th 1867

I received duly your letter of the 16th August—and my father's. I am more gratified than I can tell that my miserable scrawls to you, continue to give you satisfaction—I can only say you are easily pleased. Your news about James is indeed very melancholy. It is quite a new thing for him to take to such things: for though he and I were sometimes delinquents while I was with you, I think he was more influenced by my example than by any desire for wildness. I trust that by this time however he has got steady: and will keep so until you decide upon what is best to be done for him. The Bank I always thought was a miserable place for him: among uneducated boors, with the most uninteresting of all work to do, and on wretched pay, I wonder that he even stayed there a month. Let me know what you are thinking of doing with him, as soon as you have made up your minds.

Willy seems to be in a poor way from your account; but the coming home may do him good in more ways than one. You may be able to get him a situation at home—and he will be obliged to work steadily, now that he has a wife to support as well as himself. On all other topics, your letter was as always, full of the most pleasant news. Everybody appears to be well, and the old people all growing young again, from what you say. The trip to the Continent will be a splendid thing for Andrew, and will put him into health and heart for his work in the winter.

November 10th or 11th?—I stopped above on account of interruption, and did not resume till today. You will have got no letter from me by the last Mail: for the following reason. Our examination came on in the last week of October, and I had arranged to take a few days holyday, when I had got it over. I went accordingly to "the Wall" (i.e. "the Great Wall") for a five or six day's tour, and the Mail went away in my absence. If I had heard the result of the Examination before going I should have dropped a note in before starting: so there is my excuse: and I hope you will see the force of it! Well, you will be glad to hear that the reputation of the ancient house of Porter, for literary pursuits, has not suffered in my hands. The competition was for three "Senior Studentships". The senior students are to remain longer in Peking, than those who fail to take one of the three places, that a reward may be thus offered to men who have worked hardest, and have shewn most ability in learning the language. Their salary is at the same time

increased by £100 a year; and when at length they leave the capital to
do duty in the ports, they are moved one step beyond what they would
have been had they not acquired the distinction. Without further
preface I may as well tell you that I came out *first*: to my own very
great surprise, although I have since found that a good many of the
men expected that result. The examination lasted three days, and was
conducted by Mr Brown, Chinese Secretary. Mr Hart of the (Chinese)
customs was also present, having been asked to assist him—and also
a native scholar, formerly teacher to Mr Wade—in the presence of the
great Sir Rutherford Alcock. The first day a Despatch was served out
to us all, which we were to translate before twelve o'clock next
day—with the help of our teachers, dictionaries, and in fact everything
but the assistance of any European. It was by no means a difficult paper,
and was done, I understand very well by everybody. The second day
was oral examination—reading aloud, translating, and answering
questions on the text. The third comprised more reading, a series of
questions on the government of China and such like: writing Chinese
sentences from dictation—(a most awfully difficult thing) —and oral
interpretation. The result of all this was—I was first: a man called
Baben second, and McKean third. The latter was at a considerable
disadvantage, having been obliged to do work for the accountant all
summer, while the latter was at Shanghai with the Chief. I thoroughly
believe all McKean's pleasure at seeing me first was greater than at
finding himself one of the lucky number. This last examination now
nullifies the order of precedence established by the previous one before
the Civil Service Commissioners, and consequently puts me over the
heads of three or four men who were over me.

I am glad that after telling you that I was working steadily, I am
able to confirm my previous reports of myself by the news of the result
of this examination. Don't blame me, if I have blown my own trumpet
a little lustily. If I don't, no-one else will. Besides you will be glad to
hear from myself all about myself.

So now, I may expect to be here for another year, and I am on the
whole glad that it is to be so. I am moved into the office of the Chinese
Secretary where I see a good deal of the manner in which business is
carried on with the Chinese Government. When I am some time there,
I shall now and then have the translating of some despatches, and there
can be no better practice. I have besides to translate the Peking Gazette
every morning for the Chief who gets it at lunch time to read.

My box arrived here safely on the 8th of November, having been
only a little over two months on the journey. Many thanks for the

trouble you took in getting the things—and for the socks which you sent me yourself. The hat and pants fit capitally: but Mr Arnold must have some confused idea that it is to my Uncle William at the Cape he was sending the white drills, for they would certainly fit the limbs of that great man.[1] That can be easily remedied however. Thank Sandy for his little volume of poems which I have not yet had time to read. When I have done so, I shall write to him and thank him myself. Don't understand by this, that if on reading they don't answer expectation, I shall not write to him!

November 20th—Another interruption having taken place, I did not resume till today. Your Mail of the 20th September has come in, telling of James' steady behaviour while with Johnny. I have not the least doubt that he will now keep so; and that he may get a good situation I earnestly hope. You must let me see some of Andrew's letters from the Continent; they are always good reading: and now that he is on the spree as it were, they ought to be doubly amusing.

Three new students arrived here safely the other day, and brought safely your splendid present. You could have sent me nothing that would have pleased me better: for though I have out here opportunities of reading the book, it is one which one would like to have always at hand. Thank my father and dear Maggie most affectionately for their share in the gift, and accept my dear Mother, my warmest thanks for yours. I have a number of things which I mean to send home in the spring to you: little things in porcelain and so forth, which I pick up, bit by bit. You wrote to me some time ago that you thought the Chief could [get] a box sent home for me. He has got no more power to do so than I have: indeed less: for at a port I might ask a captain to carry a box for me *gratis*: but he with his great salary could scarcely do so. But Bismarck, Secretary in the Prussian Legation (a nephew of the Count), is going home as soon as the river opens, and will take a box for me.

The cold is now intense; with a wind from the North East enough to skin a fairy. I find my pea-coat about the most comfortable thing that I could have got. Indeed it is quite warm enough to wear without a fur lining. Altogether I am most comfortable. I will try to tell you some *news* by next Mail. Meanwhile, love to all including James from,

Ever dearest Mother, your loving son

---

1 He was six feet two inches tall.

To his Father

British Legation, Peking—December 8th 1867

I have not written to you for a long time, having always *addressed* my letters to my mother; but indeed change the address and the same letter would do equally well for either. My last letter will I am sure have afforded you great pleasure; not from the fact of my having surprised a few other men in my studies, but as being a witness to corroborate my own statements—often repeated to you, that I had been working regularly and living steadily. Since my examination I have not been doing much beyond my ordinary routine in the office—translating the Peking Gazette every day, and now and then a despatch. You may be interested in knowing what is the nature of the News-medium called a *Gazette* by us. It is written by hand, and consists of three distinct parts, "The Court Journal", never larger than a slip of paper, about eight inches square, which contains generally any news of public ceremonies, to be performed by the Emperor, or those deputed by him, a list of official announcements of the reports of different Boards to the throne; and is moreover the medium by which officials return thanks for their appointments. This is always a separate slip. The other two parts are bound up, or rather stitched up, each forming a separate little book, averaging generally from 20 to 30 pages each; but this number varies of course with the amount of official information to be conveyed. One is the Decrees *from* the Throne; the other the Memorials presented to it. The work is not issued by any office in the state; and contains no more information than it chooses shall appear in public. It is conducted by a private firm, which gets the documents from the clerks and underlings in the offices on duty in the palace, and who copy it for sale. Printed copies are then struck off; but are so badly done that by any one but a Chinaman they are almost illegible. We take in the Manuscript copy which cost $8 a month; while the printed ones can be had for four *tiao*, about half a crown a month. To conclude: both are turned out on paper of a straw colour, and the consistency of silk-paper.

I think I mentioned that I am going to send home a box in the early spring by a friend of mine here, who then goes home on leave of absence. Don't expect anything grand. I have some pretty pieces of old and new porcelain in different forms; and I shall put in some few wearable(?) furs which however with some few exceptions are as dear here as at home. Your books and some gazettes (which I shall translate) will go with the other things. Since I last wrote, a very good piece of news has been announced here. The Chinese are about to send a diplomatic Mission to the Courts of the Treaty Powers in Europe and America. They have enlisted the services of the Hon. Anson Burlingame,[1] the American Minister here, who was just returning to his own country, to act as their Minister at the Foreign Courts, and of Mr Brown, Chinese Secretary in our Legation, as first Secretary to the Mission. This is obvious as they have no one who speaks any foreign language, of sufficient rank to act in such high capacities. Several high Ministers in the state are going, accompanied by a full suite of servants, even down to the barbers! I inquired of my teacher, "*Why two?*" "Can a man shave his own head?" said he: and the reason is a good one. I suppose Mr Brown will be over in Belfast next summer, and has promised to call on you. You will find him a most excellent fellow in every way, and as well informed as any man I ever met of his age: so shew him any hospitality you can for my sake. You'll find his company will more than repay you for your trouble.

I am glad to hear from you that the meeting of the Social Science Association was such a success. The reports in the papers I suppose give a fair idea of the business done though by no means a full one. I shall be glad to see the pamphlet, containing the published account of the whole transactions, your own papers among the rest.[2]

I am not making much way at the Hebrew. I find I cannot do much at two languages together; I mean to try it just a [bit] longer and if I find I am not making progress, I shall give it up. In the latter case I shall send you back your old friend *Gesenius*; of which indeed I should never have deprived you. I have even lost almost all of any correctness (*fluency* is long gone) in speaking French, that I had. I constantly find Chinese words and phrases, cropping up at inopportune times: and indeed it would be surprising if this were not so—reading, speaking and thinking in Chinese, for more than a year and half.

But if I have forgotten other things, I have not yet forgotten you, and all the dear ones at home. Chinese can never alter *that*: and it is a dear thought to me to find that you are of the same feeling to me—all of you, as your letters shew. So now I am at the end of my paper, and

---

1 Anson Burlingame, 1820–70, United States minister to China, 1861–67, special minister to foreign powers for Chinese government 1868–70.
2 Held in Belfast in September 1867. John Scott Porter read a paper advocating undenominational education in the national schools.

my news has long been ended. Remember me to all who care to inquire after me—and with love to everybody at home, believe me,

Ever your loving son

[N.B.—This was written on his 22nd birthday: J.S.P.]

To his Mother
British Legation—January 10th [1868]

I have not a minute to spare, nor have had since Mr Brown went away a week ago, and I have no news, even if I had time to write. I received your letters, and shall answer them by the next Mail, at length. I cannot tell you how glad I am to hear of James. More by next. I am quite well: and with love to all,

Ever your loving son

To his Mother
British Legation—January 20th 1868

I promised you, I think a long letter by this Mail: but nothing has turned up to tell you. Snow has been lying on the ground for about three weeks, and skating is out of the question: the weather is however clear and bright, though terribly cold. I have no fire-place or stove in my bed-room, and the water in the jugs and bath is frozen nightly. I myself am warm enough, thanks to about two ton of clothes upon the bed. The absence of rain is the great thing that makes up for all these discomforts.

Your last letter, enclosing one from Johnny to you was very pleasant. James deserves great praise for his conduct indeed. My grand-father cannot, I am afraid last long from what you tell me of his altered state: nor indeed, is life a boon under such circumstances. I am glad though, that every one else seems to be well.

Brown started the other day with the Chinese who are going home. They go overland to Chin Kiang, a town not far from Shanghai, on the Yangtse, and thence to Shanghai. I think there are in all 39 Chinese. I don't envy Brown his trouble in looking after the stupid fools, especially when they get home. He promised me to go and see you when he went home, and please do anything for him that you can. He gave up no small portion of his time, to teach me and one or two others the language (for which he was not paid by Government), and has befriended me in fifty ways.

Another great friend of mine, Murray, is also going home in a short time, by Siberia and Russia. He lives at Stranraer; and says he will certainly cross and see you. Tell my father that he will take him home his Chinese books, and a few other little things. I cannot burden him with a big box, as they go by cart all the way to Russia: and speed will be the object this cold weather. He may probably stay a night in Belfast, in which case you might give him a bed. Brown and he have been the two best friends I made since I left Belfast. I have no more to tell you about: so farewell my darling mother: love to my father and all,

Ever your loving son

To his Mother
Peking—March 20th 1868

I can really this Mail do no more than simply tell that I am well and have received your dear letters, and a nice kind note from James. Pray thank him for it, and tell him I shall write to him as soon as I have collected materials for a letter. I really promise you a long letter by the next Mail that leaves here. Love to my father and all, and to yourself dear Mother from

Your loving Son

To his Mother
Peking—May 24th 1868

I have not had positively one moment's time, even to scrawl you a line for now two Mails past but I have in former letters told you that news is scarce here, and if I had had ever so much to tell you, I assure you I could not have made a letter to you. I have been kept close to my books and my desk for a long time, and just when I want to write a letter home, in comes a d——— (no, a *confounded*) despatch to copy, or to put *into* Chinese, or to translate *from* Chinese.

Your last Mail came all safe but brought no better news than the one before. I had long foreseen the (probably) quick death of my dear old grandfather; but I was considerably startled when the news came. By this time I hope my Aunt Eliza will have got over her grief in a great measure. Poor soul! She had much to bear the last few years; and no one could have borne it better: though few, with her constitution with half as much "*pluck*".

I am sorry to hear that poor old James, the companion of my school-boy days, and the best friend I ever had, has gone away. Yet I know you and my father acted for the best: and I am sure that to have brought him back to Belfast would have been simply his ruin. If he keeps steady, (*as I am sure he will*) he will yet be a source of pride and honour to you—my darling dear Mother, and my dear old father. God knows I love you both, if possible, better than when I left you; and would do anything for one kiss from you, and one hearty shake of the hand from him. James I have no doubt will keep steady; and if so, with his abilities will do well. I will not admit to myself that he has any innate or inherent vice. Weak he may be; but innately vicious he is not. He will prove that in the long run.

I have written a good deal about him to you, because I know how much anxiety he has caused you: but keep up your heart old woman, and trust to my predictions.

As to Johnny's kindness and generosity, I know no word sufficiently strong to express my admiration of them. He is one of the noblest fellows I ever heard of. If I ever attain to one half of his noble generous character, I shall think myself. Well, no matter what. I am proud of him, and only wish he was in a better position than he is. He deserves it: no man better.

With regard to other news your letters were very pleasant. I am not by nature particularly fond of children; but I make a decided exception in favour of Bella's; and I was glad to hear from you of the good health they were all enjoying. The Knickerbocker suit must have been a great source of delight to my old friend *Johnston Billy*; and I should think a horrible source of envy to Sandy Jim. Tell my two nieces—Theodora and Amy, that as soon as I can find time, I shall write to them in return for their nice little notes.

As regards myself, I am well; as I always am. I had grown a very respectable pair of whiskers some time ago, but I have now cut them off. I send you along with this, a group likeness of Charlie Andrews, a fellow student called Warren, and myself. It is a very bad one of me and rather worse of the two other men. My hair has turned to curl, which I cannot quite understand; but still I cannot be made answerable for the freaks of a photographer.—The group was badly posed, by a bad photographer; "et hinc illæ lachrymæ!" (You are a Latin scholar you know!)

Say to my father, that I received his letters by the last Mail, and if time allowed would answer them by this one; but a good time is in store for him tell him. I have all his letters in my desk and will not fail to answer all his queries. Tell Maggie also that I am ashamed to think how many letters (no—Essays) I owe her; but they will all come in good time. Meanwhile, I am, my darling Mother,

Ever your own

To his Mother
Peking—June 18th 1868

To repeat for the thousand and first time that your last letters were pleasant and loving, would perhaps appear absurd, if it were not true. True, your *news* has been melancholy indeed; the one death following so closely on the heels of the other; but I am sure you will—after your first burst of grief, —feel that the death of my dear old grandfather was a release that you cannot well deplore. When I said above that your letter was pleasant I did not allude to the news it contained but to your dear, loving, what I may call *chat*; for you and I write to each other just as we would converse. I confess that the last few Mails have not contained news that is much calculated to exhilarate one's spirits, or produce what may be termed joviality—but this my darling mother is the least of it. The feeling of being totally unable to render any consolation to you or to cheer you up in any way has made me chafe and fret: bite my chain as it were, to get off to you. But enough on a subject that must have cost you a sore heart already. I shall not probe the wound any longer.

I was terribly anxious about James, after I heard of his second break out; but I am now perfectly easy on that score. He will find now for the first time that he *has* to do for himself, and I feel *confident he will do it*. I am longing to hear of his arrival at his destination and all his voyage adventures. If you would, like a dear old mother, let me have his letters as they come, I promise to send them all regularly back. I enclose Andrew's from "the sunny Rhineland", which I ought to have sent before: but every time I read them, I liked them more and more. However you have them now.

I have not, I know, written so regularly of late, as in days of yore; but I have often told you why: want of—not news—but of absolutely anything to say. Even this letter cannot be a long one; for besides paucity of ideas my time has been taken up working at a translation from the Gazette about a victory over some confounded rebels in the Eastern Provinces, which the chief (as usual) sent in at the last moment, that I am cut down to only about half an hour to do my correspondence. Well, about myself, *personally* (not generally) I send you a photo of my ugly mug, taken with one of our escort, an Irishman, and a splendid fellow. I had done one or two little things for him in the way of writing letters for him and that sort of thing; and he besought me to let myself be taken in a group with him. It's not like me. I had shaved my whiskers at the time; but only think of the moustache! Give one to Maggie, the darling and keep the other. I wear the sword, in virtue of being a volunteer in case of extra service being needed for the defence of the Legation. The weather now is hot; and I am accordingly going off to the hills this week: in fact as soon as the Mail is despatched. Charley Andrews is there now, and the Chief has been out for some time.

By the way, I took the liberty of sending to Murray, that sheet of your letter in which you spoke of him; so you are tolerably sure of a visit from him. His address is "John Gillespie Murray, Stranraer". If you and my father do not find him as good and as fine a fellow as ever you saw, I'll eat my boots. Tell Polly not to fall in love with him!

And now I have exhausted my little stock of twaddle and must dry up. Love to my dear father: to Andrew and Maggie with all the rest of the Royal family; and to you, darling mother—any amount you like

Ever your loving son

P.S.—Don't laugh at the photos! they do look as if Whelan was just about to send a bullet through my brain. Never mind!—By the way I have mislaid— not lost—Andrew's letters. I'll send them next time.

To his Mother
Peking—September 8th 1868

I have not written to you for some time, but I have regularly received all your letters. I find now that when no news is to be had the writing of a letter is no easy job or I should have sent you many more epistles than I have of late. Your last one containing the copy of Willy's letter home was very pleasant indeed. He writes in good spirits and seems to be happy. No letter from James yet I suppose. Poor fellow! I hope he is doing for himself by this time. The only bad news in your last was that of Bella's ill-health; and you appeared to think there was no danger I trust she has got over her attack. I owe letters to all that household—father, mother and children; and mean to pay them off some rainy day. My next letter home will be from Ningpo: Whither I am ordered to proceed on a week's notice; I am busy packing, and what with that and paying farewell calls in all parts of the city (on *foot*, for I have no "moke") I am pretty busy just now and quite ready for my bed at night. Three men are to be sent down. I don't yet know who the other two are, nor do they, McKean who is doing Murray's work for him will be up here the winter at any rate. I shall be sorry to leave the old place and particularly now when the winter, the jolliest season here is coming on. Besides the new American Minister is coming up in a week or so, with three grown up daughters. *Eheu!* I shall miss the contemplation of their charms, and they are said to be pretty. I shall have plenty to tell you of when I get to my port; and it's my own fault then if for four or five Mails, I do not spin you a good long yarn. Address F.K.P.—HBM's Consulate, Ningpo: that's all. I hope you have seen Murray by this time. I have not had a note from him since he left Galle, on his way home. By the way did I mention to you that I had sent home some rather valuable Chinese books to my father, by a young fellow of our service, who suddenly fell into a large fortune, and went home? He was to give them to Johnny in London who would send them on to you. I had not time to attempt even a precis of the contents of either. One speaks for itself—the picture one. It appears to be a history of the cotton plant up till the time it leaves the loom. The other is in a kind of what one might call manuscript printing; printed in the characters that would be written by a very good writer.

    I send you home a very bad photo of the little temple, where Andrews and I spent some time this summer. It will give you however, a very good idea of the sort of thing a Chinese temple in the hills is. It is called Pao choo toang: the ravine of the precious pearls—Andrews and I being of course, the pearls. I expect to be able to send you home some good views from Ningpo; which I hear is a pretty place. Love to my father and all.

Ever your loving son

P.S.—I'll send home Andrew's letters from the Rhine, by next Mail.

To his Mother
HBM's Consulate, Tientsin—September 24th 1868

Here I am on my way to Ningpo, as I told you in my last letter I expected to start for soon. I left Peking on Sunday, for Tangchow, about fifteen miles from the Capital, on the river. I rode down, accompanied about half the distance by all the fellows from the Legation and five or six from the Customs. Andrews and O'Brien came with me the whole way and stayed at the inn with me that night. Next morning at day-light they rode back, and I embarked in my boat for Tientsin. I was very sorry to leave the old place, where I had found so many good and true-hearted friends—it was like taking leave of home a second time. The fellows too were very sorry to lose me (so they said) and it's always a satisfactory feeling that you have left none but friends behind you. I had a pleasant enough trip down the river, and wanted nothing but company to make it quite enjoyable. The boats are comfortable—a raised cabin on deck in which one can but just stand upright, but long enough for a bed: and a little room to spare. My servant followed in a similar boat, and cooked my meals for me, whence they were handed in to me. I have left out enough of books to keep me in reading till I get to Shanghai; so though solitary I was not alone. We stopped frequently all the way down the river to take in vegetables and fruit—as for animal food my boy had, besides meat two live fowls on board. I speedily found out from their crowing that they were both cocks; and to wile away the time, set them to fight. The details of the combat I need not relate. I had the pleasure of eating the beaten chicken that night, at dinner.

I got into Tientsin at day-light on Wednesday and at about nine a.m. went up to the Consulate. The Consul and wife were I found at Chefou on a trip; but I had no difficulty in getting rooms to put up in till the steamer started. I sleep here, and mess with an old friend of mine here. The interpreter here, who ought to have put up a man in his own service, made no offer to do so; but he is a queer fish, from all accounts and I am glad he did not. I think he meant to be hospitable, but did not know how. Let us be charitable, I have free access to the club here, which is a real blessing, for I would find time hang heavy otherwise. I can run over there at any time, and read the papers, play bowls, fives or billiards. There is always some one about the place, ready for a game.

Your Mail passed through Tientsin yesterday; but the Foreign Office bag by which your letters come can be opened by none but the Minister: McKean will send them on to me, however. I go by the steamer *Manchu*, an American Company's boat, which starts at day-break on Saturday: then I shall have had three days down here. She seems a comfortable boat, and as there is abundance of room, and but few passengers on board, I shall probably have a cabin to myself. I am taking with me a Kangaroo hound—(overhaul Peter Parley's[1] Natural History, and ascertain if that animal—the Kangaroo—not the hound, exists at Ningpo) and a little Pekinese spaniel that I was going to send home to Maggie, by Murray, if he had gone by Siberia. I may have a chance of doing so yet, as, at a port I can always find sailing ships going round the Cape; the difficulty is to find some one to look after the creature and see that it is sent on safely. More of this however in future communications.

I am to discharge the duties of Interpreter at Ningpo. As it is only an *acting* appointment, I don't draw the whole pay of the post. For the present I draw an acting allowance of £100 a year in addition to the three I already have. It is probably that I shall have a further sum of £70 as Mail agent; but that being in the gift of the Consul, some one else may hold it. If I do well at the interpreting work it will of course be so much towards future promotion: but this is speculating. Of the Consul (who rejoices in the euphonious name of *Fittock*) I know no more than that he is a good-natured fellow, and inclined to treat his juniors well: nor of his wife, than that she drops her *h's*, and has a large family of small brats. The Chief facetiously told me that one of the duties of an Assistant is to wheel the Consuless's children in a peram-bulator after office hours! "No, not for Venice!" Murray's youngest brother is in the Customs service at Ningpo—if he is anything like his

---

1 Peter Parley was the pseudonym of William Martin, 1801–67, who wrote numerous instructive books for young people.

brother he and I ought to get on well. I hope you have seen Murray before this reaches you; I am anxious to know how you and my father liked him. He told me he would write after he had seen you and as no letter has come from him since, I presume he had not gone across at the date of the last Mail. I must now dry up my narrative which I shall resume when I arrive at Ningpo, giving you an account of my voyage from this place with all the flirtations and love-makings incident thereto.

October 15—I have several times attempted to resume my narrative but have always been interrupted by something or somebody. I am now at Ningpo, and am at present staying with a Colonel Cooke, Commandant of the Chinese Contingent and head Superintendent of Police. Fittock has not yet arranged about quarters for me; and a new Consulate is in process of building. In the meantime I draw $45 per month, till the Government provide me with quarters. I also draw £70 a year as Mail agent, so that altogether I am now pretty well off.

I cannot keep my word about giving you all the details of my voyage by this Mail; but look out for it by the next. *"Shall I lay perjury upon my soul?"*

Your last Mail arrived with letters from my Father, Drums and Polly, I am glad to hear good accounts of Bella. Theordora will keep you amused during the winter; and among ourselves, the little thing will enjoy it more than staying at home—for I am afraid Bella rather cottoned to Amy: yet "I would not hear her enemy say so."

I cannot give you many details of this place yet, but when I know more of it you shall. I send you two photos of my ugly mug which were taken by a Major Watson here. They are anything but good: but I don't care. You would like anything that bore even the faintest resemblance to *"Fass"*. Tell Maggie on the word of honour of a gentleman, and an officer receiving the Queen's pay that my hair was not curled artificially when my phiz was taken. It was cut very short, and curled naturally after a cold bath. I am, dearest Mother,

Ever your loving Son

8 'The Chinese embassy in London: *Illustrated London News*, 3 October 1868. The *News* reported: The group we have engraved contains the portraits of the Hon. Anson Burlingame, Envoy Extraordinary and Minister Plenipotentiary of the Chinese Empire, and of the associates, secretaries, and attachés of his Legation, numbering twelve gentlemen besides himself, including two European secretaries. Mr Anson Burlingame is a citizen of the United States of America, and was

Minister of the United States Government at the Court of Pekin from 1861 to 1867. . . . [He] was one of the chief promoters of a beneficial change of policy in that empire with regard to foreign nations. On his retirement from the American diplomatic service, . . . he received from Prince Kung, the Regent, an unexpected invitation to become the representative of the Empire of China in a special mission to the Governments of Europe. Mr Burlingame, in the group we have engraved, appears standing in the middle. The First Associate Minister, Chih-u-Kang, sits at his left hand, and the Second Associate Minister, Sun-Chia-Kung, sits at his right. The former, otherwise called Chih-Tajen, or his Excellency Chih, is a Mantchu Tartar, fifty years of age, a man of great learning and political experience, who has also done good military service. The other, Sun-Tajen, as he is usually called, is likewise a great scholar, but has served the Empire in a civil and military capacity, and has held the office of one of the Imperial Censors, whose duty it is to remonstrate against any wrong acts of the government. The European gentlemen, seated on each side, next to the Associate Ministers, are Mr John M'Leavy Brown, the one to our right hand, and M. Emile Des Champs, to our left hand. Mr Brown, who is First Secretary of this Legation, is an Irishman, born near Belfast, and educated at Queen's College, Belfast, and Trinity College, Dublin. In 1861, he obtained by competitive examination, the appointment of a student-interpreter in the British Consular Service in China. He was, for eighteen months, private secretary to the late Sir Frederick Bruce, then British Minister at Pekin, and was acting Chinese secretary during nearly five years. He has latterly, with the consent of the British Foreign Office, been attached to the present Chinese mission in Europe . . . The other members of Mr Burlingame's party are Fung-Yeh and Teh-Ming, the Lao-Yeh, English interpreters; Kway-Yung, Russian interpreter, and Tah-Key-Che-Na, or Moo-An, Russian interpreter; Lien-Fang, or Choon-Tsing, and Tien-Kien, or Foo-Cheu, the two French interpreters; Chaung-Chou-Ling, or Soong-Joo, and Koug-Ting-Yung, or Yean-Noong, the scribes.

To his Father

HBM's Consulate, Ningpo—October 31st 1868

Many Mails have come and gone since I last wrote to you but this time I can acquit my conscience of anything like wilful neglect. I have had a busy time of it since I came here. What with learning the work of the office, all of which, Chinese excepted was new to me—calls on the Chinese officials and the foreign residents I have had little time to spare: not enough at all events to write anything like a *letter*. After having made my own calls on the Chinese authorities, Fittock came back from Japan: and I was obliged to go with him again—then the calls were returned: and all that takes up some time; for I must be in readiness at a moment's notice, to interpret for him.

So far I have got on well: and if there is not a great press of work, I shall have to work at my Chinese even in office hours. I have been reading some of the analects of Confucius, and some other standard works, and I am now at work on a translation of a Chinese drama, which I shall read at the Literary Society of this place; and if the audience receive it favourably, and if I think it of any literary merit, I may get it into some of the Magazines. At all events the work is of use to me, should it not fetch a halfpenny; I shall send you a translation of it, or at least the original, and you can have it copied. I have no one here either to help me with the Chinese, or to copy.

In health, thank God, I am well—never better—and the place agrees with me wonderfully. I am still staying with Colonel Cooke. He is the only officer of Major Gordon's Anglo-Chinese force (that fought against the Taipings) who was retained after that body was disbanded. I am not, of course, preying on his hospitality, for I am a regular member of the mess. In the meantime I draw $45 per month, of house-rent, till the government supply me with a place of residence.

I'll try and give you an idea of the business of the place. Every nation represented—that is to say—every nation that has a treaty with the Chinese has a Consulate at the port. Then there is the Office of the Commissioner of Customs (under Mr Hart)—the Chinese Officials with whom we come immediately in contact are—the *Taotai* (or Intendant) the *Chih-fu* (or Prefect), the *Chih-shien*'' (or sub-prefect)— for Ningpo is a *fou* (prefectural city); and there are some smaller ones whom we scarcely ever see, and who transact business with us through their superiors. Public questions, to and from the Authorities, are transmitted in the regular despatch form: private ones take the form of semi-official notes, written on red paper. I have to translate and answer all such; and if the *taotai* takes it into his head to make work, I am the sufferer. Often however I simply read my despatch to the Consul, and make my translation at my leisure. The outgoing despatches I draft myself, Fittock telling me briefly what he wants me to say. I keep the accounts of the place, and manage the working of the Mails, for which last I receive £70 a year. It is not hard work—but it obliges me to be up once or twice a fortnight at 6 in the morning—and in winter that is not so very pleasant.

The people here, are very nice, so far as I can see. Mrs Fittock is a charming little woman and sings like a *hangel*! She has not got the "omnibus hoc vitium est, inter amicos", etc., etc. and is always ready to perform. Tell my mother that there is a very pretty girl here whom I love very dearly!

Your last Mail went of course to Peking, and will come down in due course—but I cannot answer any queries therein proposed.

But enough of the first personal pronoun: tell me when you write how every one is, and particularly how Bella is getting on. I am writing to James: in fact I have written: but the letter has not yet gone. I hope he is doing well. I am sure if he does, he *must* get on. If he had only come out to our service, he and I might have been together. Who can tell?

With my dearest love to my Mother, and Maggie and all, I am my dear Father,

Your loving son

To his Mother

HBM's Consulate, Ningpo—January 2nd 1869

I have absolutely no more time than just to tell you that I am in good health: and that I have passed a thoroughly miserable Christmas. More anon. Work is heavy and as the Chinese (which all devolves upon me) is pretty stiff just now, I am kept busy. With my very best love to you all, and wishing you all the compliments of the season, I am my darling dear Mother, Ever your loving Frank.

P.S.—Tell dear Maggie that I received her *Muffetees*, and have worn them ever since. I wish to God I was with you all this Christmas; but

I hope and mean to be before long.—My exile is growing totally intolerable. Whether it is that I want a wife, or what I know not; but I am rather homesick. Good bye; and God bless you all

Ever your loving son

To his Mother

HBM's Consulate, Ningpo—January 14th 1869

I had made up my mind to send you a long letter by this Mail; but I have nothing whatever to say: and as your last Mail did not arrive, I have nothing to answer. The bag is opened now at Shanghai—(it used *not*) and my letters sent down to me: so I suppose your letters must have been posted late. I got my papers however. I am still dodging on in the same way as when I last wrote—a good deal of work but not so much as to prevent me from getting a little quiet time here and there for a little Chinese—though I am not doing much of it now—just keeping up what I have until business is slack, I think I told you I was living in a pretty Bungalow on the river: the rent of which is defrayed by Her Most Gracious Majesty.

I live here and mess at the Customs with Murray's brother and one or two other nice young fellows, four of us in all. It saves me a great deal of bother and expense, besides the wretched loneliness and forlornness of my condition, if living all alone I should either take to strong waters, or opium—or commit suicide inevitably. I am delighted to hear that Andrew's little affair is likely to come off. I hope the mainspring is as nice as she is made out to be by the glowing imagination of her ardent *lovier*. What about a wife for me? Has Johnnie any matrimonial matters on hand? or Drummond?

You are quite right about Brown. He is a more solid man than Murray; and though possessing all the other's goodness of heart, he is not so likely to take one's fancy in so short a time: but a better fellow never lived.

I am, I need not say, looking anxiously for the missing mail; as well for the news it is sure to contain as that it will give me some matter to work upon when next I write. I send my father a letter I wrote long ago [of 31st October 1868; see above] but it is as true now as then. Love to all

Ever your loving son

To his Mother

HBM's Consulate Ningpo—March 27th 1869

I duly received your last long long letter (my Mails now come to me
direct, not through Shanghai); and I was glad to hear you were all so
well. I suppose Andrew[1] is spliced by this time: give me all the
particulars of the wedding; and in fact all about it, him and her. I have
little to say in the way of news, for the place is at present dull—so don't
look for anything of that nature. I am writing to Johnny; whom I admit
I have treated shamefully; but I hope to make it all right with him. I
owe Polly many essays: they are in the press! though not on the shelf.

I am getting on well here and hard at work on a Chinese novel. It
is awfully dry and childish, except where it is obscene; and that is not
seldom; but I learn a good deal from reading it; and occasionally enter
into long and deep discussions on different topics as they arise. Chinese
Buddhism is at present our game—about which I am trying to get some
little reliable information; but the man is a Confucianist; and I must
take his statements, with a very large grain of salt.

I have had pleasant letters both from the Chief and Lady Alcock
who don't seem to have forgotten me. The old lady had sustained a
great loss by the death of one of her favourite dogs, and was inconsolable.
Miss Lowder is well: (I am not in love!) I had a long letter from Jack
Murray telling me of his brother's death. He seems terribly cut up about
it, and writes in low spirits. He says he has been unwell "and had at
one time a kind of hope that he was on the point of learning the great
secret: but Azrael Consolator swept past to others more worthy of the
knowledge, and left him unsaved." This is not a healthy tone of mind
for so young a man. You must ask him to Belfast again. He is loud in
praises of you all.

Nothing but rain for the last month but today seems more hopeful:
and I am going up country with Murray Jun.[r] to spend Easter Monday:
not with rolling of eggs however; except down my own throat.

I must write to Johnny though: so goodbye. Love to my father and
Bella, Maggie, Drums and all: and believe me

Ever your loving son, Frank.

FINIS!

1 He married Agnes Adinston Horsbrugh on 12 April 1869.

APPENDIX

Before the letter of the 27th of March 1869 reached the fond Mother to whom it was addressed, the sad intelligence had reached us that our darling Frank—our joy, our pride, our hope—had been taken from us by an untimely death. It was in the month of May 1869 that the melancholy tidings reached me. I was then in Birmingham on public business; and was the guest of my old and steadfast friend, Mr Joseph Chamberlain,[1] formerly of London, to whom—as he and the family and some friends were one afternoon engaged in friendly converse—a telegram was handed, the perusal of which produced a marked change in his countenance, and whole appearance. I saw at once that it brought intelligence of a deeply painful character. I exclaimed, "Joseph, my dear friend, that telegram brings sad tidings!" "Yes," he replied, after a short pause, "most distressing tidings; but to you more especially. It relates to a member of your own family; and it will require all your fortitude to enable you to bear the tidings like a man." After having thus, in some measure, prepared me for the contents of the document, he handed it to me. It was from my son-in-law, Alexander O.D. Taylor of Belfast, asking Mr Chamberlain to inform me that a telegram, sent by Mr McKean of the British Legation in Peking, and forwarded by way of St Petersburg, had been received in Belfast, conveying the sad news that my darling son Frank had unfortunately been drowned at Ningpo—whilst bathing, on Easter Saturday the 3rd of April. The information was far too circumstantial, to leave any room for doubting its accuracy. I instantly hurried home to Belfast, to do what I could to comfort by my presence and my sympathy the fond mother and the loving brothers and sisters under the sad trial, thus suddenly laid upon us. It was an arduous duty that was thus thrown upon one who needed the strength and comfort which he was called upon to impart: but not so arduous as it would have been but for the meek and gentle spirit, which, blessed be God! reigned in the breasts of all: and most of all in the breast of her who stood most in need of its strengthening support.

1 Father of Joseph Chamberlain, the Victorian-Edwardian statesman and himself a leading Unitarian and liberal.

The fragmentary reminiscences of the childhood and infancy of her darling son will have sufficiently shewn how near his loved image lay to her maternal breast—and the letters above copied manifest that her glowing affection was fully reciprocated by him who was its object. It is with a view to preserve in my family some memorial of the feelings of both these beloved ones—now alas! removed—that I have transcribed the foregoing pages into the present volume.

In due time communications were received from Mr Fittock, Her Majesty's Consul at Ningpo, and also from Mr McKean of the British Legation at Peking, which unfold all the particulars of the melancholy tale. I append these documents without alteration or abridgement.

J. Scott Porter

Lennoxvale, Belfast—August 1879

1. *Letter from W H Fittock Esq., Her Britannic Majesty's Consul at Ningpo, in the Empire of China*

[To Revd J. Scott Porter]
British Consulate, Ningpo—April 8th 1869

Reverend and Dear Sir,

It is my painful duty to communicate to you the melancholy intelligence of the death of your son, Francis, who was unhappily drowned, whilst bathing on the 3rd instant at a place named Tsing ling du, about five miles from Ningpo.

The accompanying copy of the depositions of two of poor Frank's companions at the time of the sad occurrence, will serve to acquaint you with the particulars in detail of the painful event, and I need only add here that at half past four on Saturday last the 3rd instant, your son, accompanied by his intimate friends, Messrs D'Arnaux and Preston of the Imperial Customs and Mr Brown, a merchant of this place, started in boats on an excursion up the river. All went well with the party until bed-time, when Frank stated his intention of taking a bath before turning in, "as he always slept better afterwards"; his friends endeavoured to dissuade him, but unfortunately he would not be guided by them. He undressed, splashed into the water alongside the boats, and presently after a cry for "help" was heard. Unhappily this could not be rendered in time; and the conclusion is that being seized with cramp, he must have sunk at once; his body being carried away by the strong undercurrents.

Every effort has been made to recover the body; but up to the present time I am sorry to say without effect. I shall address you again by next Mail on this painful subject; meanwhile it will be some consolation to his parents, and relatives and connexions to know that Mr Porter's untimely end is deeply deplored by all who knew him at the Post; and it is with the most unfeigned grief I have to forward you the sad intelligence of your bereavement.

I am, Reverend and Dear Sir,
Your Most Obedient Servant,

[Signed] M.H. Fittock, Consul

Revd J. Scott Porter,
Pastor of the 1st Congregation
of Protestant Dissenters, Belfast

2. *Deposition of A.N. Brown, Esq. relative to the death by drowning of F.K. Porter, late Acting Assistant and Interpreter in Her Majesty's Consulate, Ningpo*

At HBM's Consulate at Ningpo, the sixth day of April in the year of our Lord one thousand eight hundred and sixty nine, personally appeared before me—HBM Consul for Ningpo in the Empire of China, Alexander Nairne Brown, who having been duly sworn deposes as follows:

I am a partner in the firm of Davidson & Co. About 1/2 past 4 o'clock on Saturday the 3rd instant, I started in company with Mr Porter, Mr Preston and Mr D'Arnaux on a trip to the interior in the direction of You You. We had three Boats: one my own house Boat and two China Boats. Preston and I occupied my Boat and Porter and D'Arnaux one of the China Boats; the other being used for Coolies etc. Some delay took place soon after starting owing to Preston's shooting some teal, so that we did not get to a place named Tsing ling du, only about 15 li from Ningpo, until over 7 pm. We had commenced dinner before I noticed that the Boats had stopped. After finishing dinner we all four sat down in my Boat talking for some time. At the close of evening (about 10 p.m.) Porter and D'Arnaux went to their own Boat, leaving Preston and myself lying down reading. Shortly after, Porter called out that he was going to take a bath as the evening was hot and sultry and he would sleep the better. I told him I thought he was foolish. Shortly after, I saw him cross my boat naked, going to the Cook-boat on the upper side of my boat, it being ebb tide at nine. I called to him to take a rope and he answered back, "that is just what I am looking for." I heard him jump into the water, and immediately after went to the front of my own Boat, when I saw D'Arnaux hastening to the other end of the Cook Boat, but did not feel any cause for anxiety when of a sudden I heard the word *"Help!"* which sounded down stream, slightly below the boat on the other side of mine. I recognized the voice as being Porter's: and he must have swam or been carried from the place he went into the water, round the other two boats. I then hastened to the end of the Cook-boat but could do nothing. The Boats were immediately loosed and turned downstream in the direction the cry had come from. D'Arnaux had pulled off his clothes and wanted to jump in; but I advised not to until we could see or hear something to guide him. After searching for some time, we brought the boats back to the original spot; and despatched D'Arnaux to Ningpo to communicate the sad event. Preston and myself then landed and walked down the bank of the river with a lamp; but we saw or heard nothing further. I have stated that I saw Porter passing my boat naked—this was the last I saw of him. He was perfectly sober and in good spirits. The day had been very warm; and as Porter spoke so confidently of the bath doing him good before turning in, I did not anticipate any actual danger. I heard the splash when he went into the water; and it could barely have been a minute before I heard the cry for help. My impression is that he was taken with cramp and sunk instantly.

[Signed] A.N. Brown

Sworn before me at the time and place first above written

[Signed] W.H. Fittock
      HBM's Consul

3. *Deposition of George D'Arnaux relative to the death by drowning of F.K. Porter Esq., Assistant and Acting Interpreter, HBM's
   Consulate, Ningpo*

At HBM's Consulate at Ningpo, the sixth day of April in the year of
our Lord one thousand eight hundred and sixty nine, personally
appeared before me HBM Consul for Ningpo in the Empire of China,
George D'Arnoux who having been duly sworn deposes as follows:

I am a Frenchman, and employed in the Chinese Customs Service.—
On Saturday the 3rd inst. about 1/2 past 4 p.m. I started in Company
with Mr Porter, Mr Brown and Mr Preston on a trip up Country in the
direction of You-You. We proceeded on our way without anything
particular occurring, except some delay whilst Mr Preston landed to
shoot some teal. About 5 minutes to seven I ordered dinner, and a short
time afterwards the boats stopped on account of the ebb-tide making.
There were three boats: Mr Brown's Houseboat and two China-boats.
Mr Brown and Mr Preston occupied the Houseboat, Mr Porter and I
one of the China-boats, the other being used as a Cook-boat. After
dinner we all sat talking until about 1/2 past nine, when Porter and I left
for our own boat to undress for bed. During the evening we had been
talking about having a swim the next day as the weather was warm and
sultry and the water getting nice and clear. After I had undressed, Porter
said he should take a bath, before turning in. I tried to dissuade him,
not fearing any particular danger, but because the evening was dark. I
remarked it would be much better tomorrow. I went to the House-boat
to get a light for a cigarette, and on returning I saw Porter coming from
our boat, without any clothes on. He said he was very warm and should
take a bath. I remarked that it was very foolish. He persisted in his
intention, and stepped on to the fore-part of the House-boat. I heard
Mr Brown recommend him to take a rope. I also advised him to take
a rope; but he replied, "I am a good swimmer, and only intend to take
a dip." We both stood on the front of the boat together, and he again
asked if I would go in with him: but I said "No: certainly not," it was
too dark and cold. I then saw him splash into the water. He neither
dived nor jumped. He had previously asked me if I thought the water
was deep there; and I answered I did not think so as the bow of the
boat was resting on the bank. When he got into the water he began to
swim; but I noticed the current was very strong, as he was going
downwards instead of up, although his action was upwards. The tide
was ebb at the time. I still did not think there was any danger, but held

held out my arm remarking that the tide was very strong and he had better swim round the boat and land. For some time I heard his splash in the wake and then the sound ceased, and I jumped into the cabin of the House-boat, saying I was afraid something had happened to Porter. We all hurried out, and I distinctly heard a cry for "Help!" The voice was Porter's: but I think he must have had water in his throat. I wanted to jump overboard to go to his assistance, but was dissuaded by Brown and Preston, as we could neither see nor hear anything. Immediately afterwards, the boats were cast loose, and we proceeded to search for our companion, but without effect. I then volunteered to come to Ningpo to report the sad occurrence, leaving Brown and Preston with the boatmen to prosecute their search. I can swear positively that Mr Porter was perfectly sober and in good spirits. We none of us thought anything serious would come of his taking a bath before going to bed; but at the same time we all thought it was not wise for him to do so; the evening being rather dark, although sultry. My conviction is that he was seized with cramp, soon after he got into the water, and was drowned in consequence.

[Signed] G. D'Arnaux

Sworn before me, at the time and placed first above written

[Signed] W.H. Fittock, HM Consul

4. *Letter from W. H. Fittock Esq., HBM's Consul at Ningpo, to the Rev. J. Scott Porter, Belfast*

To Revd J. Scott Porter
British Consulate, Ningpo—April 19th 1869

In continuation of my letter of the 8th inst communicating to you the sad intelligence of the death of your son Francis, I have now the melancholy satisfaction to be able to inform you that the body was recovered on the 14th inst and that the funeral took place on the 15th.

It was of course incumbent on me in my official capacity to take charge of your son's effects: and to file claims against the same; and I regret to have to inform you that the latter will seriously predominate over the proceeds of the former. I have however considered it consistent with usage to allow Mr Murray, your son's most intimate friend, to select such books and other articles from the effects as he may consider might be acceptable at home; and about these things he will personally address you. The gold chain, studs and links which your son was using at the time of his death, I inclose herewith, together with three letters received by last Mail.

I have the honour to be,

Reverend and Dear Sir,
Your Obedient Servant

[Signed] W H Fittock, HM Consul

5. *Letter from Edward McKean, Esq., Attaché of the British Legation, Peking*

To Revd J. Scott Porter

British Legation, Peking—18th April 1869

Fearing lest you may not have been written to from Ningpo of poor Frank's untimely death, I have taken upon myself to send you the full particulars as they reached this [place] yesterday. I can add nothing to the information which the inclosed papers furnish.*

I do not venture to intrude upon the sacredness of your sorrow for the loss of a son so affectionate whose thoughts ever since the day he left his home were rarely separated from those with whose welfare he associated every earthly happiness.

During his residence here he made many friends to everyone of whom yesterday's news brought unfeigned grief.

I have written to Mr Fittock, the Consul at Ningpo, and have given him your address. I requested that he would send you direct every information which may be obtained, with respect to the recovery of his remains. I will myself send you copies of all the papers which reach the Legation: and if there be any service which it is in my power to render, I trust you will not forbear to write and request it. Poor Frank and I were known to each other over six years and a half: and from the day we left Southampton in company, until his departure from Peking, we had been to each other as brothers.

Deeply sympathizing with Mrs Porter and Yourself in this your great affliction, I remain my dear Mr Porter,

Yours very sincerely,

[Signed] Edward McKean

[*NB   These papers were exact transcipts of the Depositions given above: J.S.P.]

6.   *Second Letter from Edward McKean, Esq., of the British Legation, Peking*

To Revd J. Scott Porter

Peking—September, 26th 1869

I received your letter of May the 19th some time since, and I derived some satisfaction from learning that the Telegram of April the 23rd which I sent, was intelligible when it arrived. We feared lest by some mistakes of the Russians, which are not uncommon, the sadness of the news might have been intensified, if that were even possible. As regards its cost, that was by Sir Rutherford Alcock's directions included in the public accounts. But I trust you will not think that I would not have borne any expense willingly, rather than have felt that I had left anything undone, which it is the simple duty of all, circumstanced as we are here, to do to the relatives of our friends.

Mr Fittock has I doubt not settled poor Frank's affairs, and communicated with you. I know from letters that have come to Peking, that a monument has been erected over his grave, by his friends. I have tried to obtain a drawing of it; and should this reach me, I shall send it to you.

I think I mentioned to you in my last letter, that Frank had left behind him in Peking, some books and some other articles which I collected, and would have sent to him by an opportunity I had early in the year, but that I met with an accident in riding on the very day that I intended to have packed them, these I have now packed in a small tin lined box which I purpose to send to Shanghai, and to have shipped to your address by a sailing vessel round the Cape. As for the gun and the revolvers which he brought from home, I think he had sold them previously to his departure from Peking, where such articles are useless, and to keep them in order requires care and trouble. His watch was so broken upon one occasion, that being no longer of use, he left in my care until he might be leaving Peking, since my boxes were more secure; but upon the day of his leaving we both forgot about it. So soon as I am ready to send the box, I will write again sending a list of its contents.

M. D'Arnoux is at present in Peking and has asked me for your address. He says that he obtained a negative of a photograph of Frank which was taken in Ningpo, and that he sent it to his father to have copies printed in France, and these he is anxious for his father to send to you.

I hope you will write to me if there remains anything you would like me to do. It was Frank's desire to have sent to you much of the curious things to be found here; and his taste enabled him to discriminate really fine specimens. Should you desire any articles that he may have ever mentioned, which it may be in my power to procure—or if you have any wish which I am able to accomplish you will do me an injustice if you refrain from making it known to me. It would be an unworthy end of all our friendship if regard for his Memory did not sway me even more than this.

Begging that you will express to Mrs Porter my most earnest sympathies, I remain, Dear Mr Porter,

> Yours very truly
>
> [Signed] Edward McKean

[It seems only necessary to add to the foregoing that the box of which Mr McKean makes mention in the foregoing letter was by him duly forwarded. It contained several articles in Jade, Agate, Ebony and Porcelain—which in the opinion of good judges bear out the favourable estimate that he gives of poor Frank's taste as a collection of specimens of Chinese art. To the same gentleman, the family are indebted for a photograph and also a pen and ink sketch of the Monument erected over the grave of my beloved son; as well as for several other marks of kindly sympathy.—J.S.P.]

BIBLIOGRAPHY

Banno, Masataka, *China in the West, 1858–1861: the origins of the Tsungli Yamen* (Cambridge, Mass., 1964).

The book of the fete, 29 May–1 June 1907, Queen's College, Belfast (Belfast, 1907).

Belfast Directory, 1960–69.

Cambridge History of China, ii, Late Ch'ing 1800–1911, ed. John K. Fairbank & Kwang-Ching Lui (Cambridge, 1980).

Cameron, Nigel, *Barbarians and Mandarins: thirteen centuries of Western travellers in China* (New York & Tokyo, 1970).

Cox, E.H.M., *Plant-hunting in China* (London, 1945).

Deane, Arthur, ed., *The Belfast Natural History and Philosophical Society Centenary Volume, 1821–1921* (Belfast, 1924).

Dictionary of National Biography.

Fairbank, John King, Bruner, K.F., Matheson, E. MacL., eds., *The I.G. in Peking. Letters of Robert Hart, Chinese Maritime Customs, 1868–1907*. 2 vols.

Hsii, Immanuel C.Y., *China's entrance into the family of nations. The diplomatic phase, 1858–1880* (Cambridge, Mass., 1960).

Jamieson, John, *The history of the Royal Belfast Academical Institution, 1810–1960* (Belfast, 1959).

McCracken, J.L., *New light at the Cape. William Porter, the father of Cape liberalism* (Belfast, 1993).

Mackerras, Colin, *Western images of China* (New York, 1991).

Memorial addresses and sermons occasioned by the deaths of Rev. John Scott Porter and Hon. William Porter (Belfast, 1880).

Northern Whig (1860–1869).

Patton, Marcus, *Central Belfast, an historical gazetteer* (Belfast, 1993).

Rockhill, William Woodville, *Diary of a journey through Mongolia and Tibet in 1891 and 1892* (Washington, 1894).

Woodcock, George, *The British in the Far East* (London, 1969).

INDEX

8   The monument to Frank Porter
mentioned on page 155